Gourmet FISH ON THE GRILL

More than 90 Easy Recipes for Elegant Entertaining

PHYLLIS MAGIDA *and* BARBARA GRUNES

CB
CONTEMPORARY
BOOKS

CHICAGO

Library of Congress Cataloging-in-Publication Data

Magida, Phyllis.
    Gourmet fish on the grill : more than 90 easy recipes for elegant
entertaining / Phyllis Magida and Barbara Grunes.
        p.   cm.
    Includes index.
    ISBN 0-8092-4596-5 :
      1. Cookery (Fish)   2. Barbecue cookery.   I. Grunes, Barbara.
II. Title.
TX747.M239   1989
641.6'92—dc19   88-38225
                                          CIP

Published by Contemporary Books, Inc.
180 North Michigan Avenue, Chicago, Illinois 60601
Manufactured in the United States of America
Library of Congress Catalog Card Number: 88-38225
International Standard Book Number: 0-8092-4596-5

This book is dedicated to our two wine consultants,
Leonard Solomon and Shawn Magee,
both of whom helped us to bridge that mysterious gap
between wine and food.

Contents

Introduction   1
Ingredients and Equipment   4
Menu Planning   14

1   **APPETIZERS**   18

2   **ENTREES**   26
   Fish
      Catfish   26
      Cod   31
      Flounder   36
      Halibut   44
      Mackerel   48
      Mahimahi   56
      Marlin   58
      Monkfish   60
      Ono   64
      Orange Roughy   65
      Pompano   72
      Red Snapper   74
      Rockfish   86
      Salmon   89
      Scrod   94
      Sea Bass   100
      Shad Roe   101
      Shark   102
      Sole   104
      Swordfish   110

Trout   114
Tuna   124
Turbot   128
Whitefish   131
Leftover Grilled Fish   142

Shellfish

Shrimp   146
Soft-Shell Crabs   150
Stone Crab Claws   152
Mixed Shellfish   154

3   SIDE DISHES   156

4   DESSERTS   170

Appendix: Mail Order Sources of Ingredients
      and Equipment   181
Index   182

Introduction

In the last few years more people have been preparing fish for themselves and serving it to guests than ever before, probably because of increased concern about calories and cholesterol. Nevertheless, a major complaint heard again and again at self-help weight-loss groups is that going to someone's house for dinner is always fattening and unhealthy. Many hosts, it seems, are still serving rich, heavy meals to their guests.

French gourmet Jean Anthelme Brillat-Savarin used to say that when you invite someone to dine you charge yourself with his or her happiness. If only hosts would remember that the definition of happiness today—at least at a dinner party—means going home without being angry at yourself for eating too richly and without feeling logy and stuporous from eating too much.

For our third fish grilling book (the first is called *Fish on the Grill* and the second *Shellfish on the Grill*) we've created and double-tested more than 90 recipes, including 7 luscious desserts. This book is intended for entertaining, so most of our recipes serve eight, rather than the usual six, and they can easily be cut in half to serve four.

In most entree recipes, we call for 3 pounds of fish—roughly 6 ounces of raw fish, which will end up as 4½-5 ounces cooked, per person, which should be more than enough. However, if you've invited guests with really healthy appetites, increase our suggested amounts to 4 pounds to allow each guest 8 ounces of raw fish or somewhere between 6 and 7 ounces cooked.

We've also included suggestions for what to serve with the recipes. You'll note that green salad is usually mentioned. This isn't because we were lazy; it's because grilled fish and green salad go so well together. And we've included extensive directions for setting up an elaborate salad bar for entertaining (see Chapter 3).

And for those hosts who have trouble planning menus, we've included a discussion of how to do so effectively.

You'll note that we suggest margarine as an alternative to butter in almost every recipe. In cases where you really feel the dish will suffer greatly from the substitution, we suggest you mix the two or buy one of those butter/margarine combinations now commercially available.

Each recipe contains a suggested substitution for the fish that it calls for. We urge you to be creative and to remember that most fish and their sauces—not just the ones we suggest—can effectively be interchanged.

Because of the emphasis on entertaining in this book, we worked extensively with three consultants: fish expert and retailer Louie Green; wine consultant, author, and retailer Leonard Solomon; and wine teacher and sommelier Shawn Magee. Our fish expert has detailed some important things to understand when buying fish that is to be cooked on the grill. And he's created a special chart for us—one we've never seen before in any fish book—that suggests, among other things, cooking times for different varieties of fish to be cooked on the grill.

Our wine consultants worked long and hard to come up with just the right accompaniments to grilled fish dishes. See their general comments linking wine with grilled fish in "Menu Planning."

As we noted in our earlier books, fish cook quickly on the grill—especially the thin, delicate fillets that should not be turned—so we strongly urge you to *watch* the fish carefully as it cooks. The difference between a perfectly cooked fillet that has just turned opaque and a dry-textured, overcooked one is often just a moment. Luckily, whole fish and thick fillets take longer and can be dealt with in a slightly more casual fashion.

We are introducing a method of cooking delicate fillets—the ones that cannot be turned—that we developed as we worked on this book. Cook each fillet on ¼-inch-thick orange or lemon slices or use slices of vegetables such as onion, pepper, or eggplant to protect it from direct heat.

We also suggest trying a new product called the Griffo-grill (discussed in "Ingredients and Equipment"). It fits right on your barbecue, preventing small fish pieces from falling through to the coals below. And it acts as a heat buffer as well.

We combed the globe to find recipes and flavors that are interesting, unusual, and fast and easy to prepare. Then we adapted them to suit the tastes of Americans and to call for ingredients available in this country. In this book we think we've succeeded in bringing you the best that many cuisines have to offer. You'll find recipes for everything from exotic Moroccan dishes like Monkfish with Cracked Green Olives and Red Snapper with Marzipan to more familiar-sounding dishes such as Catfish with Mexican Red Sauce and Orange Roughy with Black Butter Sauce (see Index). We hope you will enjoy each one of our recipes—at least as much as we enjoyed creating them for you.

Ingredients and Equipment

HOW TO BUY FISH

Almost any kind of fish can be put on a barbecue grill. The first consideration is what kind of fish to buy.

When making this choice, don't be limited by preconceived ideas as to what you *have* to have for dinner. Be flexible; keep your options open. Don't say to yourself, "I just have to have swordfish tonight, no matter what!" First see what looks good. If what you had in mind doesn't appeal to you, don't buy it. Don't be talked into something you don't want. Most reputable fishmongers will steer you in the right direction. Make sure your local purveyor knows your likes and dislikes.

It's not difficult to learn to identify truly fresh fish. If it's fresh, fish will have:

- clear, bulging eyes
- shiny, elastic skin
- red, clear gills
- a clean, fresh smell
- bright red, not brown, blood (if any)
- a clean and clear color for white-fleshed fillets, a rich color for dark-fleshed fillets

If possible, avoid precut steaks and ask your fishmonger to cut them as you need them.

Fish fillets should not have direct contact with ice; ice water breaks down protein in the flesh and results in a loss of flavor and quality.

After making your selection you need to know how much fish to allow per person. Here are some general guidelines:

- whole fish (as caught, viscera intact): 1¼ inches thick or 6 ounces per person
- whole dressed fish (head on, viscera removed): ¾–1 inch thick or 8–12 ounces per person

- fish steaks (round slices, horseshoe-shaped, bones intact): 6–8 ounces per person
- boneless fillets and steaks (such as swordfish, tuna, marlin, and shark): 6–8 ounces per person

A point should be made regarding inconsistencies in the size (market weight) of whole fish. There are legal limits relating to the minimum size of the catch, but there is no limit on how big the fish can be, so steaks of a certain thickness can vary widely in weight, depending on the size of the whole fish. For example, a 1-inch-thick salmon steak cut from a 3-pound sockeye salmon would weigh 6–8 ounces, but a 1-inch-thick steak cut from an 18-pound salmon would weigh 12–16 ounces. To get what you want; let the fishmonger know your intentions for the fish—how many people you are serving and whether they are adults or children, as well as what type of preparation you have in mind. Then let the fishmonger make suggestions. If the thickness of the cut is altered drastically because of the size of the fish, merely adjust the cooking time.

HOW TO COOK FISH ON THE GRILL

Once you've decided on the variety and cut, you must contemplate the method/technique to be used in cooking. Considering the choice you've made . . .

Is the fish firm enough to place directly on the grill? Halibut, swordfish, tuna, and grouper are a few examples of fish that can go directly on the grilling surface with little or no risk of falling apart.

Would the fish be better off grilled in a basket? Fillets of whitefish, lake trout, salmon, red snapper, or sea bass—thin or delicate, flaky-meated fish may be better in a basket.

Would a bed of citrus or vegetables be more suitable? Delicate, thin fillets, such as sole, flounder, small red snapper, pompano, and sea bass benefit from this method.

Can the fish be threaded on a skewer? Swordfish, tuna, and rolled fillets of salmon can be skewered, as can shellfish such as sea scallops and shrimp.

Now that you've made your selection and chosen the cut and technique, we can move to preparing the grill.

Whether you are using a gas or charcoal grill, preheating is very important. Using a cold grilling surface can cause problems in properly cooking your fish.

For gas grills: Preheat at a high temperature for 10–15 minutes. Use a brush to remove old barbecue sauce, food, and grease stuck to the surface. Turn the temperature down to medium heat. The grill is now ready to use.

For charcoal grills: Unless you're steaming a large whole fish, a single layer of coals across the surface of the charcoal rack will suffice. Spray the coals with lighter fluid. Using tongs, stack the coals into a pyramid and spray briefly once more. Allow the fluid to be absorbed into the coals for 5–10 minutes, then light them. Carefully replace the grilling surface over the flames to sanitize and burn off charred remains. When the flames die down and the coals are white-hot, remove the grill surface and use tongs to rearrange the coals in a configuration that combines the direct and indirect cooking methods, as described below.

For *direct cooking method* the coals are concentrated under the food, throwing heat directly upward to cook the food at its highest accumulated temperature.

In the *indirect method* the food is surrounded by heat. Stacking the coals in layers around the perimeter of the grill, with the cover down, allows the heat to circulate for more even cooking.

For the *combination method* a few coals are spread directly under the fish, with some stacked around the perimeter of the grill. This gives you the best of both cooking methods.

If the fire is too hot, you run the risk of drying the outside of the fish before the inside is cooked. Remember, it is always better to undercook than to overcook. If the fish is not done when you take it off the grill, you can always put it back on. If it's overdone, there is no second chance—the fish will be dry, probably fishy-tasting, and definitely not as enjoyable as it otherwise would be.

Fish flesh sticks to metal, so don't forget to oil your fish well on both sides, to oil the grill, to oil the inside of the grill basket, and to insert lemon or lime slices at a few places between the fish and the grill when feasible.

The variables in cooking fish on the grill are innumerable. Common sense and trial and error play an important role in mastering fish grilling techniques.

LOUIE GREEN'S FISH AND SHELLFISH GRILLING CHART

Louie Green, our very knowledgeable fish consultant, is fish and shellfish manager/buyer for three large Chicago-area gourmet shops called Foodstuffs. He was literally born into the fish business—his father was a fish wholesaler, retailer, and consultant to the industry for many years—and has himself been in the wholesale/retail business for the last 17 years. Grilling is one of his favorite methods of seafood preparation.

This chart (see pages 8–10) includes most of the seafood included in our fish and shellfish books, except for seafood that is already cooked when purchased. The cooking times given for fish are for *boneless fillets*. The *shellfish* section of the chart indicates whether the cooking time is for shellfish in the shell or out of the shell. As we have specified for the recipes in this book, the fish and shellfish in this chart are to be cooked on a preheated grill about 5 to 7 inches from coals that have partly turned to ash.

When that fish is cut into fillets (versus steaks or whole fish), the fish's texture and density will determine whether the fish can be turned without falling apart or should be cooked only on one side. See the key at the end of the fish section of the chart for advice on turning fillets, skewering, and so on. Virtually all fish steaks can be turned on the grill, but, as we note in our recipes, any *whole* fish weighing more than 1 pound should *not* be turned, or it will fall apart.

FISH ON THE GRILL

FISH	SIZE VARIANCE	TEXTURE	MARKET FORM	COOKING TIME IN MINUTES	COMMENTS
Bluefish	¾-15 lbs.	Oily, fat, dark, firm	Whole, steak, fillet	Steak—about 6 Fillet—about 4	Excellent on grill. Mild yet distinct texture and flavor. *See Legend: 2*
Catfish	10 oz.-4 lbs.	Fat, firm, mild	Whole, steak, fillet	Steak—about 5 Fillet—about 3	Most catfish are farm-raised, making for good value and excellent quality. *See Legend: 2*
Cod Family: Cod (Scrod), Haddock, Pollack	1½-15 lbs.	Lean, firm, flaky	Whole, steak, fillet	Steak—about 6 Fillet—about 3	If skin is off, should be put on vegetables or citrus or wrapped in foil. *See Legend: 2, 3*
Flatfish Family: Sole (Grey, Lemon), Flounder (Blackback, Fluke)	½-8 lbs.	Lean, crisp, delicate	Whole, steak, fillet	Steak—about 6 Fillet—about 2	Thicker steaks/fillets can go directly on grill. *See Legend: 3*
Grouper	3-30 lbs.	Fat, firm, coarse	Steak, fillet	Steak—about 10 Fillet—about 6	Very versatile fish. Can go directly on grill; can be skewered. *See Legend: 1, 4*
Halibut	10-250 lbs.	Medium fat, firm, coarse	Steak, fillet	Steak—about 8 Fillet—about 6	Fabulous grilled. Serve hot or chilled. *See Legend: 1, 2, 3, 4*
Lake Trout	3-15 lbs.	Fat, flaky	Whole, steak, fillet	Steak—about 8 Fillet—about 4	Very tasty. As good as salmon, but less expensive. *See Legend: 2, 3*
Mackerel: Boston, Spanish, Kingfish, Ono	¾-40 lbs.	Fat, oily	Whole, steak, fillet	Steak—about 8 Fillet—about 4	Nice grilling fish. Dark-fleshed, tasty. *See Legend: 1, 2, 3, 4*
Mahimahi: Dolphin	4-25 lbs.	Fat, coarse	Fillet	Fillet—about 4	Excellent grilled as simply as possible. Delicate taste. *See Legend: 1*
Monkfish	3-20 lbs.	Lean, light texture	Fillet	Fillet—about 6	Sometimes sold as "Poor Man's Lobster." *See Legend: 1, 4*
Orange Roughy	2-6 lbs.	Lean, light texture	Fillet	Fillet—about 4	Almost always skinless; can be very delicate. *See Legend: 3*
Pompano	¾-3 lbs.	Fat, flaky, mild	Whole, fillet	Fillet—about 3	Very light, delicate fish. *See Legend: 3*
Redfish	2-20 lbs.	Fat, flaky	Fillet	Fillet—about 4	Very popular in Cajun dishes; needs seasoning. *See Legend: 2, 3*
Red Snapper: American, Caribbean, Yelloweye, Yellowtail, Silky, Mutton, Mangrove	¾-20 lbs.	Fat, rich, flaky	Whole, fillet	Fillet—about 4	One of the largest family of fish. Varieties are pretty much interchangeable. *See Legend: 2, 3*

FISH	SIZE VARIANCE	TEXTURE	MARKET FORM	COOKING TIME IN MINUTES	COMMENTS
Rockfish: West Coast Snapper	3-6 lbs.	Fat, flaky	Fillet	Fillet—about 3	Can be substituted for Red Snapper. *See Legend: 3*
Salmon: Silver, Sockeye, King, Chum	Farm-Raised, 8 oz; Wild, up to 20 lbs.	Fat, rich, flaky	Whole, steak, fillet	Steak—about 8 Fillet—about 4	One of the most popular fish anywhere. Year-round supply. *See Legend: 1, 2, 3, 4*
Sea Bass: Black, Striped, etc.	15-20 lbs.	Fat, white meat, flaky	Whole, steak, fillet	Steak—about 6 Fillet—about 4	Sea Bass refers to a large number of fish. Many varieties may be substituted. *See Legend: 1, 2*
Shad	2-10 lbs.	Fat, oily	Whole, fillet	Fillet—about 4	Very bony! *See Legend: 3*
Shark	4-200 lbs.	Lean, firm	Steak, fillet	Steak—about 8 Fillet—about 4	Meaty, mild taste. Great marinated. *See Legend: 1, 4*
Smelt	1/10-1/4 lbs.	Crisp, lean	Whole	Whole—about 3	*See Legend: 3, 4*
Swordfish	20-200 lbs.	Fat, rich, firm	Steak	Steak—about 8	The King of the Grill. Cooks like meat. These steaks are boneless. *See Legend: 1, 4*
Tuna	10-500 lbs.	Oily, fat, rich	Steak, fillet	Steak—about 5 Fillet—about 3	Outstanding on the grill. Very tricky. Must be cooked like rare steak. Steaks are boneless. *See Legend: 1, 4*
Turbot	3-15 lbs.	Lean, rich, delicate	Fillet	Fillet—about 3	Like Orange Roughy; always skinless. Very delicate. *See Legend: 3*
Whitefish: Lake Superior, Canadian	1½-10 lbs.	Fat, rich, flaky	Whole, steak, fillet	Steak—about 8 Fillet—about 4	Delicious on the grill. Can be delicate. *See Legend: 1, 4*

LEGEND:

1. Can be put directly on grill and handled like meat.
2. Larger, thicker pieces can be put directly on grill.
3. Delicate; should be put on bed of vegetables, herbs, or citrus slices and not turned.
4. Can be skewered.

PLEASE NOTE:

* Cooking times are approximate.
* We have not given cooking times for whole fish as whole fish vary greatly in size.
* Cooking times for fillets are for those fillets placed on citrus slices or vegetables and not turned over. (Fillets are never turned over unless they are more than 1-inch thick.)
* Cooking times for steaks are given for 1-inch thick steaks.

SHELLFISH ON THE GRILL

SHELLFISH	SIZE VARIANCE	TEXTURE	COOKING TIME IN MINUTES	COMMENTS
Clams in Shell	Medium or small clams are best for grilling	Tender	About 6	Optimal size to use are Topneck, Small Cherrystones, or Littlenecks.
Crab: Dungeness in Shell	1¼-4 lbs.	Tender firm	About 7*	*Most often crabs are precooked, so just heat.
Crab, Legs and Claws: King Crab Legs, Snow Crab Claws	1-4 oz.	Tender firm	About 3	Both King Crab Legs and Snow Crab Claws are available frozen and precooked.
Crab: Soft-Shell	3", 4", 5", 6"	Tender/ crisp	3"-4"—about 4 5"-6"—about 6	Although grilling is not the most popular preparation, Soft-Shells are great grilled. Extremities crisp up and bodies and claws stay moist.
Crayfish, Whole	12-40 per lb.	Tender firm	About 4	Size dictates cooking time. Large Crayfish are more desirable for grilling.
Lobster Tails: Australian, New Zealand, Bahamian, Japanese, Honduran, Danties	2 oz.-2 lbs.	Tender firm	About 18 per lb.	To prepare for grill, remove undershell by cutting up sides with kitchen shears. Remove meat by separating, wedging fingers between meat and shell at top of tail and working back, leaving tail attached. Push meat back in tail. Cook ⅔ time on shell side, ⅓ on meat side.
Lobster, Whole, in Shell: Maine, Spiny	1-6 lbs.	Tender firm	About 10 per lb.	Can be par-cooked 2-3 min. on stove to kill lobster. Should be turned halfway through grilling.
Mussels, Skewered: Maine, New Zealand	Small, 1"; med., 1½"; large (greenlip), 2"	Tender	About 3	Can be bought already shucked or can be removed from shell after grilling.
Scallops, Bay: Calico, Florida	40-70 per lb.	Tender	About 4	Skewered or put on a screen.
Scallops, Sea	8-20 per lb.	Tender	About 8	Need delicate care on the grill. Turning often prevents overcooking and drying.
Shrimp: Prawns, Scampi	2-200 per lb.	Medium firm	About 4	Bigger is not better. Ideal size to go directly on grill is 15-20 count; skewered is 36-40 count.
Squid Mantles, Skewered	3"-12"	Medium tender, chewy	About 5	Quick cooking is essential.
Squid Steaks	4-12 oz.	Slightly chewy	About 3	Prepounded from large squid. Ideal for fast grilling.

Tips for Grilling Fish

1. Remember that the fish will continue to cook after it is removed from the grill. If the fish is almost done when you test it, that's the time to take it off.
2. When cooking flaky-meated fish that you've put directly on the grill, use two long spatulas to remove the fish from the grill and to turn it.
3. Testing for doneness is crucial. One method is to insert a bamboo skewer: if it penetrates the meat easily, the fish is done. Practice by piercing the fish when raw for comparison.
4. How you place the fish on the grating is also very important. Putting the fish perpendicular to the grill bars minimizes sticking. Never attempt to remove the fish from the grill surface by running the spatula across the grill bars. This will break up the flesh and cause the fillet to separate.
5. When cooking fish with the skin left on, which is always desirable, cook the meat side first to braise and seal in juices. Then turn to cook on the skin side. Cooking fish on the meat side for one-third of the cooking time and on the skin side for two-thirds of the cooking time usually keeps the fish moist.
6. Lean fish, such as sole, flounder, bass, and orange roughy (those with less than 2 percent fat) are better if basted with some liquid or brushed with fat or oil during grilling. They are also enhanced by rich sauces. Moderately fatty fish, such as cod, snapper, grouper, and halibut (those with 2–6 percent fat) and fatty fish, such as salmon, mackerel, and whitefish (those with more than 6 percent fat) may be grilled without basting, although they are still improved if basted with liquid or brushed with fat or oil during cooking.
7. Lean, moderately fatty, and fatty fish are all enhanced by the addition of an oily marinade, such as our Basic Marinade (see Index).
8. When using wooden barbecue skewers, soak them in water for 1 hour before using to prevent them from scorching on the grill. Wooden toothpicks should be soaked as well. (Note: Round wooden toothpicks are better than flat ones for skewering.)
9. Most fillets should not be turned on the grill, or they will fall apart. Very firm fillets—those that can be turned without worry, such as

swordfish and shark—are the exception to this rule. Carefully follow our directions about whether to turn fillets.

10. When grilling delicate fillets, you can ensure that they don't stick to the grill by grilling each atop two lemon, onion, or orange slices. Discard the slices after grilling.

11. To facilitate removal of fish after grilling, oil your grills well and use two spatulas to carefully lift fillets to a serving platter.

12. Instead of chopping scallions or chives, use scissors to snip them into tiny pieces.

13. For recipes that call for chopped onion, you can determine whether you have enough onions on hand by weighing them:
    - 1 1¼-ounce onion yields ¼ cup chopped
    - 1 3-ounce onion yields ½ cup chopped
    - 1 11-ounce onion yields 1⅓ cups chopped
    - 1 13-ounce onion yields 2 cups chopped

14. Although fillets sold in fish stores and supermarkets are supposed to be free of bones, they often are not. Run your fingers up and down the length of the fillet to feel for bones before you marinate or cook the fish. If you find bones, use tweezers to remove them.

15. Lay lemon slices over each side of a whole fish when putting it into a grill basket to ensure that the fish doesn't stick. Be sure to oil the grill basket beforehand as well.

16. Save the instructions that accompany your grill and any other grill equipment you purchase. You'll want to refer to them several times as you refine your grill techniques.

17. Take care of the bottom of your grill. Line it with heavy-duty foil before adding the charcoal briquets. When you finally need to empty it—and you will be able to grill several times before you do—simply pick up the foil and discard it. This way, you won't have to turn the grill upside down to clean it. The foil protects the bottom of the grill as well.

GRIFFO-GRILL

One particularly effective piece of equipment for grilling both fish and shellfish is a stainless-steel wire rack called a *Griffo-grill*. It fits directly on the grill and is so close-meshed that it provides maximum support for delicate seafood while allowing juices to drip through. Even a bay scallop won't fall through. The Griffo-grill measures 11" × 11" and will fit on almost any size grill. It can be oiled lightly before each use to prevent fish from sticking to it. Fish fillets turn more easily on this grill, and spatulas are easily used. One of the ends is folded up to a 1-inch height to function as a spatula stop edge.

The Griffo-grill is available in many hardware shops and supermarkets, as well as in gourmet cookware shops, but if you cannot find it in your area, you can send for it. The grill sells for $9.95, but if you order it by mail, enclose an extra $2 for shipping and handling. Send your name and address, written clearly, along with a request for the grill and a check for $11.95, to Griffo-grill, 301 Oak St., Quincy IL 62301. Your grill will arrive within two weeks.

A second Griffo-grill, recently put on the market, has two handles and an ultra-heavy-duty frame and measures 12" × 16". It sells for $39.95, which includes shipping.

Menu Planning

In the late 1950s and early 1960s it was easy—even for inexperienced brides—to cook the perfect dinner for guests. It usually consisted of six courses: cocktails and potato chip dips, shrimp cocktail, lettuce with bottled dressing, giant steaks or a large roast beef served with baked potato and sour cream, green bean/mushroom soup casserole, and a dessert that was usually cake and ice cream with chocolate sauce, followed by the candy someone had brought to the hostess.

The rationale for this meal was simple: everyone liked and expected it, and it was considered fancy, which meant expensive enough to serve to guests. It was considered healthy and well balanced too in those days before we were concerned about cholesterol and weight-watching.

Today, few of us—certainly not those who think about health—would serve such a fat-laden dinosaur. Our tastes have changed, too. As we've traveled in other countries or eaten in the ethnic restaurants that have opened up in profusion around the country, our palates have become more sophisticated and our tastes more exotic.

Therefore, a whole new set of menu-planning rules has to be considered when planning a dinner party. Some have to do with nutrition; others, stemming from the *haute cuisine* of the past, have to do with flavors, textures, and presentation. Still others have to do with the sophistication of today's guests. With this in mind, we've assembled a few loose rules you might want to consider the next time you're having company for dinner.

1. Serve what the nutritionists call a balanced meal, consulting the USDA nutritional guidelines if necessary. If possible, avoid weighing a menu too heavily on any one side of the basic food groups. Balanced meals include raw vegetables, tossed with unsaturated or monosaturated oils; some protein such as fish; a side dish of bread, potatoes, noodles, or rice; and perhaps a cooked vegetable such as asparagus, green beans, brussels sprouts, carrots, or cauliflower. You might decide to serve fresh fruit with simple cookies—at least some of the time—rather than rich desserts. (We've included recipes for some desserts as well as grilled and fresh fruit selections, so you can take your choice.)

2. Keep these "gourmet" rules in mind when planning:
   - Include within one meal dishes at all different temperatures: hot, cold, and room temperature.
   - Foods within a meal should be as varied in texture as possible, from soft and pureed to slightly chewy to crunchy.
   - Try to include all of the tastes—salty, sweet, sour, bitter, bland, and even piquant—within one meal. If you're at a loss for a way to add the bitter taste, remember that coffee, grapefruit, eggplant, and beer are all considered bitter foods.
3. Keep the colors of your proposed dinner in mind, making everything as bright as possible. Bright green vegetables, colorful sauces and garnishes, and multicolored condiments all make the final plate beautiful. Try not to serve white fish on white plates. Fish is more appetizing when set on a plate of an attractive, contrasting color.
4. One semiobsolete gourmet rule advises against serving the same food twice within a meal. While you may not want to serve two sauces within a meal (sauces can be fattening), and you may not want to repeat strong flavors (such as anchovies in the salad and anchovy sauce with the fish), there's no reason why you can't begin a meal with a simple fish broth, them move to a fish entree. Here your instincts should guide you.
5. Most important, find out beforehand what kinds of food your guests like and serve those or similar kinds of food to them. If you're inviting guests who say they hate fish but like beef, try serving swordfish, which has a texture similar to that of beef and a bland taste, or serve shrimp or lobster. Or course there are always a few folks who don't like fish no matter what, so it doesn't hurt to have a steak you can throw on the grill in emergencies. Your guests should always come first.

WINE TO ACCOMPANY GRILLED FISH

Our wine consultants, Shawn Magee and Leonard Solomon, have shared their expertise with enthusiasm, suggesting the best wines (or other beverages when wine is inappropriate) to accompany each fish and shellfish recipe.

Shawn Magee on Wine with Fish

Shawn Magee has been wine director for Le Cochonnet, a French bistro in Chicago, for 2½ years. Magee teaches wine appreciation at the Cooking and Hospitality Institute of Chicago, Inc. (CHIC), and has her own consulting company, Triangle Wine Consultants.

Magee stresses that, besides the taste and texture of the fish and sauce, a wine consultant must take into consideration the cooking method when choosing the right wine for fish. "Since grilled fish have more flavors, due to the grilling methods, they require a different wine—one that is stronger-flavored or more full-bodied in texture," she says. "The same care must be taken when choosing a wine to accompany a strongly flavored sauce—a Mexican or southwestern sauce, for example, or one that is East Indian, since these sauces could easily overshadow many wines."

Wine suggestions made by Shawn Magee are followed by her initials, *S.M.*

Leonard Solomon on Wine with Fish

Leonard Solomon ("I was born in 1921—a great year for wine.") has been a wine retailer, lecturer, author, and consultant since 1945. Currently he is president of Leonard Solomon's Wines & Spirits in Chicago.

Solomon has been a forerunner of wine and food trends since he started in the business. "It's true that the traditional matchups of wine and food did actually come about because of compatibility, throughout generations of food and wine preparation. But the new cuisines demand new wine responses," he says. "Generally speaking, I feel white wine should go with fish because the structure of red wine—it contains elements like tannin and other chemicals—creates incompatible flavors when combined with fish oils."

But things are changing, he explains: "Some wines are made using cold fermentation methods, and some are not aged in oak. Because of these new methods—many of them from countries all over the world—new kinds of wine are now available. Some of them are red, and many of these would be very compatible with grilled fish."

Wine suggestions made by Leonard Solomon are followed by his initials, *L.S.*

RECIPES FOR ENTERTAINING

We have organized our book by meal course—appetizers, entrees followed by our favorite grilled side dishes, and desserts. In the entree chapter the recipes are listed by type of fish and shellfish. Each recipe gives a list of serving suggestions that best accompany the type of fish you are preparing. These range from salads and vegetable side dishes, to fresh breads, fruit dishes, and desserts. Also listed are suggestions for fish substitutions just in case your local fishmonger has run out of your first choice. Our wine consultants have recommended the perfect wine to complement each meal, and these are listed at the end of each recipe.

Above all, we've meant for this cookbook to inspire you to be a little more creative in preparing elegant meals for your family and friends. We hope you'll have as much fun as we did in developing this cookbook for you.

1
Appetizers

COLD HALIBUT HORS D'OEUVRES WITH WHIPPED CREAM MUSTARD

This yummy appetizer can be made with any fish that is delicate in flavor but strong enough to hold together when speared with a cocktail toothpick.

FISH
1 recipe Basic Marinade (see Index)
2 pounds halibut fillets, about ¾ inch thick

WHIPPED CREAM MUSTARD SAUCE
1 cup whipping cream
2 tablespoons Dijon mustard
1 tablespoon white vinegar
1½–3 teaspoons sugar (to taste)
¼ teaspoon salt (more to taste)

1. Marinate the fish: Place the marinade in a large plastic bag, add the fillets, and secure with a twister seal. Turn the bag several times to make certain all fish surfaces touch the marinade. Set the bag in a bowl and let sit at room temperature for 1 hour, turning the bag occasionally.

2. Grill the fish: Remove the halibut from the marinade, place the fillets on the prepared grill and cook for 3–6 minutes. Turn the fillets carefully and cook until the fish has lost its translucence.

3. Transfer the fillets to a platter (do not use metal), cover, and refrigerate until well chilled. Then cut each fillet into bite-sized chunks. Arrange the chunks carefully on a large platter.

4. Make the sauce: Whip the cream until stiff. It will double in volume, making 2 cups of whipped cream. Stir in the Dijon mustard, vinegar, sugar, and salt, mixing well. Taste and adjust seasoning, adding more sugar or salt if desired.

5. Either serve chunks of fish topped with dabs of sauce or follow the directions below for using a pastry tube to pipe stars into a bowl or onto the fish chunks. Provide cocktail picks for guests.

TO PIPE STARS OF SAUCE

1. Drop a large star tip into a large pastry bag and squeeze it until it is tightly in place. Half-fill the bag with whipped cream mustard sauce. Then give the bag a good shake so that no air holes remain. Tightly roll up the open end of the bag.

2. Hold the bag so the tip is just barely touching the bottom of the serving bowl or the top of a fish chunk. Use your left hand to hold the tip in place so it touches a flat surface and use your right hand to hold the folded top of the bag closed tightly and to exert squeezing pressure at that end.

3. Exert slight pressure with the right hand for an instant to squeeze out a star, lifting the bag slightly but not removing it from the star. When the star is formed, lift the bag completely. Then, if piping stars into a bowl, make another star right next to the first one. Fill the bottom surface of the bowl with stars. Then make a layer of stars on top of the bottom layer. Then make another layer of stars over the second layer. By the time you are finished making your third layer of stars, you will have the hang of it. Continue piping layers of stars until the bowl is completely filled. If piping stars directly onto the fish chunks, continue piping stars until all the chunks are decorated.

Makes 8 appetizer servings

Serving suggestions: This is a rich appetizer. All other dishes—whether a main course or additional appetizers—should be lean in taste and texture. A plain fillet, first marinated in our Basic Marinade (see Index), then grilled, along with French bread and a green salad, would be ideal.

Fish substitutions: monkfish, scrod

Caution: Do not serve red wine with this appetizer. Due to the oiliness of the whipping cream and the fish, the tannin present in red wine would cause the combination to taste most unpleasant. A full-bodied chardonnay from California or Australia, rather than from France, would be ideal and would not overpower the fish. (Note: a full-bodied wine is one that gives a feeling of weight in the mouth.) *L.S.*

MACKEREL APPETIZER MARINATED IN THE JAPANESE MANNER

For this delicious Japanese appetizer, called yuan zuke *in Japan, grilling gives the mackerel skin a crisp black texture that complements the marinated fish pieces.*

MARINADE
½ cup Japanese light soy sauce
½ cup mirin (Japanese sweet rice wine used for cooking, available in Oriental food stores or by mail; see Appendix)
1 cup canned or fresh chicken broth
3 tablespoons sugar
1 lemon, cut into thin slices

FISH
2 pounds mackerel fillets with skin
Lemon wedges

1. Make the marinade: Combine the soy sauce and mirin and heat to a boil. Add the chicken broth and sugar, return to a boil, and remove from the heat. Let sit at room temperature until cool. Then pour the soy/mirin mixture into a large plastic bag, add lemon slices, and set the bag in a large bowl.

2. Marinate the fish: Cut the mackerel fillets into 2-inch pieces, each containing some skin. Place the mackerel pieces in the marinade in the plastic bag and secure the bag with a twister seal. Turn the bag several times, making sure the marinade touches all fish surfaces. Place the bag and bowl in the refrigerator for 8–12 hours, turning the bag occasionally while the mackerel marinates.

3. Remove the mackerel from the plastic bag and discard the lemon slices. Transfer the marinade to a saucepan and set aside.

4. Grill the fish: Place the mackerel slices skin side down on the prepared grill. Grill until the skin becomes crisp and black. Then turn the mackerel with tongs or a spatula and grill flesh side down for another few minutes or until the fish is lightly browned and cooked through.

5. Carefully transfer the mackerel pieces to a serving platter. Heat the marinade to a boil and spoon a little over each piece of mackerel. Garnish the platter with lemon wedges and serve immediately.

Makes 8 appetizer servings

Serving suggestions: Mild pasta, tossed with cooked vegetables, butter/margarine blend, and salt

Fish substitutions: yellowtail, ono

Why look further than a chilled or hot sake? Sake must never be served lukewarm. The tradition of the small sake cup is elegant, but a 6- to 8-ounce cup is the size required by serious sake drinkers. *L.S.*

   Note: See directions for heating and storing sake in recipe for Halibut Fillets with Miso Sauce (see Index).

CHILLED SALMON WITH RED CAVIAR MAYONNAISE

This appetizer calls for bite-sized chunks of chilled salmon to be dipped into a homemade red caviar mayonnaise. If you wish to serve it as a main dish for eight people, increase the salmon to 4 pounds and serve the fillets whole. Double the amount of mayonnaise, spooning some over each serving. The mayonnaise is made with Japanese rice vinegar because of its mildness, but plain white vinegar makes an acceptable substitute.

FISH
1   recipe Basic Marinade (see Index)
2   pounds salmon fillets, each cut ¾ inch thick

CAVIAR MAYONNAISE
1   egg
¼   cup salad oil
1½ teaspoons fresh lemon juice
1   tablespoon sugar
1   tablespoon Japanese rice vinegar
¼   teaspoon salt
¼   teaspoon dry mustard
¼   teaspoon paprika
Pinch freshly ground white pepper
⅔   cup imported mild, good-quality olive oil
2   ounces red lumpfish caviar

　　1.　Marinate the fish: Place the marinade in a large plastic bag and place the bag in a bowl. Add the fillets, secure the bag with a twister seal, and turn the bag several times to make sure all fish surfaces touch the marinade. Let sit at room temperature for 1 hour, turning the bag occasionally.

　　2.　Meanwhile, make the mayonnaise: Combine the egg, salad oil, lemon juice, sugar, vinegar, salt, dry mustard, paprika, and white pepper in a blender or a food processor fitted with the steel blade, and process for a few seconds to combine.

3. Turn the processor on and with the motor running add the olive oil in a very thin, steady stream. When all the oil has been added, turn off the motor. Transfer the mayonnaise to serving bowl. Cover and refrigerate.

4. Grill the fish: Place the fillets on the prepared grill and cook for about 4 minutes. Turn carefully with a spatula and cook for about 6 minutes. Transfer the fish to a large platter (do not use metal) and cover. Refrigerate the fish until well chilled.

5. Cut the chilled salmon into bite-sized chunks and place on a serving platter along with cocktail toothpicks. Mix the caviar into the mayonnaise and set the bowl in the center of the platter. Serve as an appetizer.

Makes 8 appetizer servings (1 heaping cup mayonnaise)

Serving suggestions: This is a rich appetizer, so serve a spartan entree, such as a plain fillet marinated in our Basic Marinade (see Index), hot French bread, and a green salad.

Fish substitutions: any type of salmon, halibut, tuna

A lot of the salmon we eat comes from the Pacific Ocean. What better accompaniment to this appetizer than Washington state chenin blanc? Or, if you serve this dish as a main course, I suggest a drier sauvignon blanc, which will not clash with the mayonnaise. Another excellent choice would be a zesty Johannisberg Riesling. The slight "spritzig" quality (spritzig, which is also know as *petillance*, is caused by very tiny, effervescent bubbles in the wine) acts as a counterbalance to the oily caviar and the slightly oily quality of the mayonnaise. The wines of Hogue Cellars, Yakima, Washington, are gold medal winners both in and out of Washington state. *L.S.*

SKEWERED FISH SAUSAGE APPETIZER

Take care not to overcook these sausages. The mixture is intentionally dry, as it has to stay on the skewers, but if it is overcooked, it will be even drier. Be sure to serve lemon wedges; the sausages need the moisture.

16   8-inch-long wooden barbecue skewers
18   ounces whitefish fillets, skinned
 4   garlic cloves, peeled and quartered
 2   scallions, cut into 1-inch lengths
 ½   cup fresh bread crumbs, ground fine
 2   tablespoons evaporated milk, half-and-half, or cream
 1   teaspoon salt
 1   teaspoon fresh lemon juice
 6   dashes Tabasco sauce
Oil for brushing sausages
Lemon wedges

1.   Place the skewers in cold water to cover and allow to soak at least 1 hour, until ready to skewer sausages.

2.   Examine the fillets carefully, rubbing your fingers up and down their surfaces to check for bones. If you find any, pull them out with tweezers. Cut the fish into chunks and place in a food processor fitted with the steel blade. Add garlic, scallion lengths, bread crumbs, evaporated milk, salt, lemon juice, and Tabasco sauce and process until the mixture is finely pureed.

3.   Scoop out 2 tablespoons of the mixture and form into a 2-inch-long sausage at the end of a skewer. Repeat with the remaining mixture. You will end up with 16 sausages, each on its own skewer.

4.   Brush each sausage lightly with oil and carefully place on the prepared grill. Grill for about 3 minutes on one side, then use a spatula to turn the sausages carefully. Grill for 3 minutes. Transfer the skewers to a serving platter and garnish with lemon wedges. Serve immediately.

8 servings (2 sausages per person)

Serving suggestions: This appetizer is spartan; follow it with a richer entree and noodles that have been tossed lightly with butter or margarine.

Fish substitutions: any dry fish—orange roughy, redfish, or walleye pike

Because this dish is similar to a Spanish tapa, I suggest serving a well-chilled Manzanilla sherry. The dish would also go well with any dry white or rosé wine mentioned in this book. *L.S.*

BASIC MARINADE

1	cup mild, good-quality olive oil
6-7	tablespoons fresh lemon juice
¼	teaspoon salt
⅛	teaspoon freshly ground pepper
2	bay leaves, crumbled
½	onion, grated in a blender (optional)
4	garlic cloves, chopped in a blender (optional)

Combine all ingredients well. Marinate 3–4 pounds of fish fillets for an hour at room temperature or for several hours in the refrigerator.

Makes scant 1½ cups (enough for 3–4 pounds fish)

2
Entrees

FISH
Catfish

Catfish is a sweet, freshwater fish. Serve it with fried onions and you're in for a real southern treat.

CATFISH WITH FRIED ONIONS

FISH
1 recipe Basic Marinade (see Index)
3 pounds catfish fillets, cut into 8 serving pieces

FRIED ONIONS
6 tablespoons butter or margarine
2 large red onions, sliced thin
¼ cup golden raisins
3 tablespoons dry white wine
¼ teaspoon salt
⅛ teaspoon freshly ground pepper
½ teaspoon caraway seed

2 oranges, sliced thin (you'll need 16 slices altogether)

    1.   Marinate the fish: Pour the marinade into a large plastic bag and place the bag in a bowl. Add the catfish, secure the bag with a twister seal, and turn the bag several times to make sure all fish surfaces touch the marinade. Let sit at room temperature for 1 hour.

2. Meanwhile, make the fried onions: Melt the butter in a skillet over medium heat. Cook the onions and raisins, stirring occasionally, until the onions are well cooked. Transfer the onions to a plate and reheat the skillet. Stir in the wine and heat. Pour over onions and combine. Sprinkle with salt, pepper, and caraway seeds. Set aside.

3. Grill the catfish: Arrange the orange slices in pairs on the prepared grill. Place each catfish fillet on pair of orange slices. Grill for 5 to 6 minutes, without turning, or until the fillets have lost their translucence and are slightly browned on the edges.

4. When the fillets are cooked, transfer them to a serving platter and garnish with the hot fried onions.

Makes 8 servings

Serving suggestions: grilled potato skins, marinated asparagus salad, cornbread

Fish substitutions: orange roughy, pollack

To complement this slightly sweet dish, choose a simple chardonnay, such as Domaine St. Georges 1985. *S.M.*

STUFFED CATFISH WITH COUSCOUS

This dish is based on couscous, grains of durum wheat semolina that are used to make the various couscous dishes of Morocco. Couscous comes in different-sized grains, any of which will work for this recipe, and is available at Middle Eastern stores or by mail (see Appendix). If desired, substitute cooked rice. Since this is a sweet couscous—one that includes nuts and currants—we've eliminated the hot sauce traditionally served with savory couscous dishes. If you wish to make this couscous savory, simply eliminate the nuts and currants and serve a side bowl of commercially available harissa *(Moroccan hot sauce), available at Middle Eastern stores or by mail (see Appendix).*

If you have a favorite chicken stuffing and wish to use that one instead of our couscous stuffing, just follow our directions for stuffing and grilling the fish. It is necessary to use a grill basket to cook a fish larger than 1 pound, or it will break when you try to turn it.

This recipe intentionally allows extra stuffing, which should be reheated and served in a separate serving bowl along with the grilled fish.

STUFFING

1½	cups water
3	cups medium-grain or other size couscous
6–8	tablespoons butter or margarine
½	teaspoon freshly grated nutmeg (more to taste)
8	scallions, green part only, minced fine or snipped fine with scissors
1	cup pine nuts
½	cup dried currants (more to taste)
1½	teaspoons salt

FISH

2	3-pound farm-raised dressed (headless, skinless, scaled and gutted) catfish

Salt and freshly ground pepper to taste
12–16   ¼-inch-thick slices lemon
Lemon wedges

1.   Make the stuffing: Heat the water to a boil and immediately stir in the couscous grains. Stir a few times, then allow to cool, stirring occasionally.

2.   Melt the butter in a large frying pan, then add the couscous grains, breaking up any clumps that have formed with your hands or with a fork. Stir in the nutmeg, scallions, pine nuts, currants, and salt and cook for 2–3 minutes, stirring constantly. Remove from the heat and allow to cool.

3.   Sprinkle the inside of each fish liberally with salt and pepper. Stuff each fish with the couscous mixture, packing tightly. Don't bother using skewers to close; the grill basket will hold each fish shut.

4.   Grill the fish: Place each fish in an oiled grill basket, placing 3–4 lemon slices on each side of the fish between the fish and the grill basket. Place the grill basket on the prepared grill and cook for about 15 minutes on each side or until the fish is cooked through on both sides and has lost its translucence.

5.   While the fish cooks, reheat extra stuffing in a saucepan, then transfer to a serving dish just before removing the fish from the grill. Carefully transfer each fish to a large serving platter and serve immediately, 1 fish for each 3 to 4 people. Pass the bowl of heated stuffing and lemon wedges.

Makes 8 servings

Serving suggestion: green salad

Fish substitution: trout

This dish has many complex flavors. I suggest an ale or even a dark beer as an accompaniment. *L.S.*

CATFISH WITH MEXICAN RED SAUCE

RED SAUCE

4   large tomatoes, peeled, seeded, and chopped
¾   cup chopped cilantro
½   small onion, minced
1   poblano chili, seeded and chopped
1   tablespoon drained capers
¼   teaspoon salt
¼   teaspoon freshly ground pepper

FISH

3   pounds catfish fillets, cut into 8 serving pieces
Good-quality olive oil for brushing fish
¼   cup fresh lime juice
½   cup minced cilantro
16   ¼-inch lime slices
2   ripe avocados, peeled and sliced

1. Make the sauce: Combine the tomatoes, cilantro, onion, chili, capers, salt, and pepper in a bowl. Cover and refrigerate until ready to serve.

2. Grill the fish: Brush the fish fillets with olive oil and sprinkle with lime juice and cilantro. Arrange the lime slices in pairs on the prepared grill. Place each catfish fillet on a pair of lime slices. Cook on the grill for about 3 minutes, without turning. Check and continue grilling for about 3 minutes, until it tests done.

3. Put the fish on a heated platter, ladle the tomato sauce next to the fish, and garnish with avocado slices.

Makes 8 servings (3 cups sauce)

Serving suggestions: warm corn tortillas, salad of lettuce with fresh fruit and pine nuts

Fish substitutions: Ocean perch, small rockfish

The freshness of the sauce, with its accompanying acidity from the tomatoes, is a perfect match for a silky bordeaux-style white from California called Carmenet, which is made from a judicious blend of sauvignon blanc and semillon grapes. *S.M.*

Cod

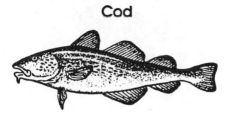

MEDITERRANEAN PITA POCKETS

EGGPLANT
1 medium-large eggplant
Salt
Good-quality olive oil
½ cup dried oregano, crumbled
2 large red bell peppers, cored, seeded, and sliced into rings

FISH
1½ pounds cod fillets
4 tablespoons fresh lemon juice
4 pita bread rounds, halved and wrapped in foil
1 cup sliced black olives

1.   Grill the eggplant: Cut eggplant crosswise into ½-inch slices. Sprinkle with salt and let stand on paper toweling for 20 minutes. Wash off the salt and pat dry. Brush with olive oil and sprinkle each slice with ¾ teaspoon of the oregano. Brush the pepper slices with oil. Grill the eggplant slices and pepper strips until done to taste. Reserve in a bowl.

2.   Grill the fish: Sprinkle the remaining oregano over the hot coals. Brush the fish fillets with olive oil and sprinkle with the lemon juice. Place the fillets on the prepared grill. Cover and grill for 3–6 minutes. Remove the cover, turn fish, and grill until done to taste.

3.   Heat the foil-wrapped pita bread on the grill, turning once.

4.   To assemble: Allow your guests to stuff their own pita pockets. Arrange the pita bread in a round basket. Cut the fish into chunks and toss with the vegetables and olives, in a bowl.

Makes 8 servings

Serving suggestions: Greek salad or deep-fried zucchini rounds
Fish substitutions: scrod, pollack
Drink a Côtes du Rhône with this casual dish. *S.M.*

COD STEAKS IN WINE WITH ROMESCO SAUCE

The delicate flavor of cod goes well with this deliciously spicy Romesco sauce.

ROMESCO SAUCE
2 large tomatoes, peeled, seeded, and chopped
4 cloves garlic, crushed
1 small dried hot chili pepper *or* ½ teaspoon red pepper flakes
4 heaping tablespoons ground almonds
¼ teaspoon salt
1½ cups good-quality olive oil
4 tablespoons red wine vinegar
4 tablespoons Spanish sherry

MARINADE
2 cups dry, red wine
1 cup good-quality olive oil
1 large onion, sliced thin
2 tablespoons chopped fresh mint
1 teaspoon dried rosemary, crumbled
½ teaspoon salt
¼ teaspoon freshly ground pepper
1 teaspoon crumbled bay leaves

FISH
3 pounds cod, cut into 8 steaks
½ cup bay leaves

1. Make the sauce: Place the tomatoes, garlic, chili pepper, almonds, and salt in a food processor fitted with the steel blade or in a blender; puree. In a separate bowl, mix together the oil, vinegar, and sherry. With the motor running, add the oil mixture in a slow, steady stream until the mixture is incorporated. Chill the sauce until ready to serve.

2. Make the marinade: Combine the marinade ingredients, pour the marinade into a large plastic bag, and place the bag in a large bowl. Place the fish in the plastic bag and secure the bag with a twister seal. Turn the bag a few times to make certain the marinade touches all fish surfaces. Let sit at room temperature for 1 hour.

3. Grill the fish: Remove the fish from the marinade (reserve the marinade) and pat lightly with paper towels. Sprinkle the bay leaves over the hot coals and replace the grill. Arrange the fish on the prepared grill and cook for 3–6 minutes. Brush with the reserved marinade, turn, and continue grilling the fish until it is cooked to taste. Serve hot with the Romesco sauce.

Makes 8 servings (2½–2¾ cups sauce)

Serving suggestions: grilled artichoke bottoms brushed with olive oil, crusty bread, fresh fruit for dessert

Fish substitutions: haddock, pollack

Torres, one of the most highly respected producers in Spain, makes a light red called Sangre de Toro, a perfect partner to the oiliness of the cod and the vinegar and sherry in the sauce. *S.M.*

COD STEAKS WITH WATERCRESS SAUCE AND WATERCRESS SANDWICHES

TOAST BASKET
Toast basket from Grilled Apple Slices in a Cinnamon Toast Basket (see Index), omitting butter and cinnamon sugar

SANDWICHES
12 slices white bread, crusts removed
 6 tablespoons butter or margarine, softened
 2 bunches watercress, stems removed, minced
 ½ cup good-quality mayonnaise

WATERCRESS SAUCE
 1 bunch watercress, stems removed
 4 tablespoons butter or margarine
 4 large shallots, minced
 2 tablespoons flour
 1 cup whipping cream
 ½ cup sour cream
Salt and freshly ground white pepper to taste

FISH
 3 pounds cod, cut into 8 steaks
Melted butter or margarine for brushing cod
Salt and freshly ground white pepper to taste
 1 teaspoon ground ginger

1. Cool the toast basket for 1 hour before serving.
2. Make the sandwiches: Cut the bread slices into 1½- to 2-inch rounds with a cookie cutter. Spread one side of the bread rounds with softened butter. Sprinkle lightly with watercress and make into sandwiches.

3.   Spread mayonnaise around the outer edges of each sandwich. Scatter the remaining watercress in a flat dish and roll each sandwich edge in watercress. Arrange the sandwiches on a plate, cover with a damp paper towel, and refrigerate for 1 hour. When ready to serve, place the sandwiches in the basket, rims up.

4.   Prepare the sauce: Blanch the watercress for 2 minutes, rinse in cold water, and drain. Pat dry with paper toweling. Puree the watercress in a blender or a food processor fitted with the steel blade, and reserve.

5.   Melt the butter in a medium saucepan, add the shallots, and sauté until tender, approximately 2 minutes. Whisk in the flour until absorbed, about 1½-2 minutes. Blend in the pureed watercress and the whipping cream; heat slowly, being careful not to boil. Remove from the heat, cool slightly, and blend in the sour cream. Add salt and pepper to taste.

6.   Grill the fish: Brush the cod steaks with melted butter and season with salt, pepper, and ginger. Place the steaks on the prepared grill and cook for 3-6 minutes on each side or until done. Transfer to individual plates.

7.   Serve the fish hot off the grill with the warm sauce and the basket of watercress sandwiches.

Makes 8 servings (3 cups sauce)

Serving suggestions: grilled cinnamon apple slices and Cotswold cheese

Fish substitutions: haddock, orange roughy

A steely Alsatian Riesling, such as Domaine Weinbach Reserve Personelle 1983, is a perfect foil for the richness of the watercress cream. *S.M.*

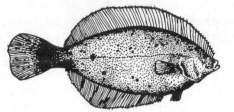

GRILLED WHOLE FLOUNDER ORIENTAL STYLE

The flounder is a mild flat fish found in both the Atlantic and Pacific Oceans.

SEASONINGS
1 tablespoon freshly grated gingerroot
3 cloves garlic, minced
1 bunch scallions, cut into 1½-inch lengths
3 tablespoons julienned tangerine peel
1 small bunch cilantro, trimmed and chopped
2 tablespoons peanut oil
2 tablespoons soy sauce
1 tablespoon Oriental sesame oil
2 tablespoons dry white wine
6 tablespoons fresh tangerine juice

FISH
2 2-pound flounders, scaled and cleaned, head and tail intact

1.   Prepare the seasonings: In a small bowl, toss the gingerroot, garlic, scallions, tangerine peel, and cilantro. Divide the mixture and lightly place one-quarter of the seasonings in each fish cavity.

2.   Heat the peanut oil in a wok or small heavy skillet. Stir-fry the remaining ginger mixture for 2 minutes or until blended; set aside.

3.   Combine the soy sauce, sesame oil, wine, and tangerine juice. Add to seasonings. Brush the flounder generously with the mixture on both sides.

4.   Grill the fish: Arrange the fish on a sheet of aluminum foil and cook for 5–8 minutes. Turn the fish carefully with a spatula, being sure not to break the fish. Continue grilling until fish is done to taste.

5.   Place the fish on a heated platter. Bring the fish whole to the table and serve hot.

Makes 8 servings

Serving suggestions: Oriental noodles with chopped scallions and minced garlic, stir-fried Oriental vegetables

Fish substitutions: Sole, sea bass, whitefish

Alsatian gewürztraminer is perfect for this dish. Look for a special bottle, Willm Clos Gaensbronel 1983 Vendange Tardive—this late-harvest wine is truly a treat. *S.M.*

FLOUNDER IN SPINACH PACKETS

These delicate green spinach wrappings not only add flavor but also protect the flounder from the direct heat of the grill. You'll find that the fish stays moist in its colorful wrapping.

MARINADE
- ¾ cup good-quality olive oil
- ¼ cup red wine vinegar
- 1 small clove garlic, minced
- ¼ teaspoon dry mustard

FISH
- 30 ounces flounder fillets (about 2½ ounces per packet), cut into 2-inch strips

SPINACH MOUSSE
- 2 cloves garlic, minced
- 1 10-ounce package frozen chopped spinach, thawed and drained well
- 1 egg
- ¼ teaspoon salt
- ⅛ teaspoon freshly ground pepper
- 4 teaspoons whipping cream

SPINACH PACKETS
- 24–36 fresh spinach leaves (about 1 pound including stems), trimmed and blanched

1. Make the marinade: Combine the marinade ingredients and pour into a large plastic bag. Add the flounder fillets. Secure with a twister seal and turn the bag several times to make sure all fish surfaces touch the marinade. Place the bag in a bowl and let sit at room temperature for 1 hour.

2. Meanwhile, make the mousse: Mince the garlic in a food processor fitted with the steel blade; add spinach, egg, salt, and pepper. Drizzle in the cream and blend.

3.   Make the packets: Lay a spinach leaf on a paper towel. Place a flounder strip in the center of the leaf (reserve the leftover marinade). Spread 1–2 tablespoons of mousse over the fish. Roll the top of the leaf to the center and bring up the bottom of the leaf, creating a package. Arrange a second spinach leaf on a paper towel and place the spinach packet in the center of the leaf. Again make a packet by folding and bringing the top of the leaf to the center of the fish and the bottom of the leaf over and around the fish. Secure the fish package with a toothpick. Use a third leaf, if necessary, to cover the fish. The ends of the fish packet can be open or closed as desired. Continue making packets until ingredients are used up; you should have about 12 packets in all.

4.   Brush each spinach packet with the remaining marinade.

5.   Grill the packets: Place the spinach packets on the prepared grill (coals should be medium-hot) or on a well-oiled grill screen. Grill for 4 minutes over medium-hot coals. Brush again with marinade, turn over, and continue grilling for 2–4 minutes or until done.

6.   If the outer leaf chars to excess, remove it before serving.

Makes 6 servings

Serving suggestions: grilled tomatoes, grilled potatoes

Fish substitutions: shark, marlin

A true Chablis, such as Laroche Grand Cru Blanchot 1985, lends additional elegance to this preparation. *S.M.*

SALMON QUENELLES IN FLOUNDER

SALMON QUENELLES

1   pound salmon fillet, all bones removed, cut into strips
2   egg whites
1   teaspoon dried tarragon
¼   teaspoon ground mace
½   cup whipping cream

FISH

8   flounder fillets, each cut into 2 horizontal strips
Melted butter or margarine for brushing fillets
½   cup dried tarragon leaves
Fresh tarragon sprigs or thin slices truffle for garnish

1. Make the quenelles: Puree the salmon in a food processor fitted with the steel blade or in a grinder. Slowly add the egg whites, tarragon, and mace. With the food processor running, add the cream in a slow, steady stream until incorporated. The salmon mixture will be delicate and light. Cover and refrigerate until ready to assemble.

2. Place a flounder strip on the work surface and cover with waxed paper. Pound the flounder thin and discard the paper. Mound about 2 tablespoons of the quenelle filling on the fillet, roll the fillet lightly, and place it on a tray, seam side down. Continue until all the fillets have been rolled. Brush with butter.

3. Grill the fish: Arrange the rolled fillets on the prepared grill or on a Griffo-grill that has been brushed with butter. Sprinkle the tarragon over the hot coals. Cook the fish for 2–3 minutes, rotate so that they will grill evenly, and continue grilling until the filling is cooked.

4. Serve 2 rolled fillets to each guest. Garnish with tarragon sprigs or thin slices of truffle.

Makes 8 servings

Serving suggestions: risotto, warm spinach salad

Fish substitution: sole

For this dish, delicate in taste as well as texture, a classic pairing would be a French white burgundy. Drinking well is the 1985 Puligny-Montrachet Clos de la Mouchère from Henri Boillot. *S.M.*

GRILLED FLOUNDER MELT

This recipe is the perfect choice for a lunch at the seashore or in your own backyard. Grilled Tuna Sandwiches (see Index) is another tempting sandwich recipe.

BREAD
2   French bread baguettes
1   tablespoon sesame seed
½   cup (¼ pound) butter or margarine, melted

FISH
Oil for brushing peppers and scallions
2   large green bell peppers, tops removed, seeded, sliced into rings
2   pounds flounder fillets, cut into 8 serving pieces
8   thin slices (or to taste) Colby or baby Swiss cheese
8   scallions, trimmed
8   crisp, trimmed lettuce leaves
¾   cup radish sprouts

1.   Prepare the bread: Slice the baguettes horizontally and cut each on the diagonal into four sandwich-sized pieces. Stir the sesame seeds into the melted butter. Brush onto the cut sides of bread and set aside.

2.   Grill the fish: Oil the pepper slices and place on the prepared grill. Arrange a slice of cheese on each fillet, trimming so that the cheese does not overlap the fillet. Place the fillets on slices of pepper and grill for about 2–6 minutes, without turning, or until fish is cooked to taste. At the same time, grill the oiled scallions until done, laying the scallions across the grill. At the same time, briefly grill (about 30–40 seconds) the cut sides of the bread.

3.   Assemble the sandwiches: Put a lettuce leaf on the bottom of each piece of bread and top with flounder, pepper, and cheese. Sprinkle with the sprouts and top with a grilled scallion. Cover with the tops of the bread and serve hot.

Makes 8 servings

Serving suggestions: potato salad, tomato slices topped with a sprinkling of balsamic vinegar and chopped fresh basil

Fish substitution: Dover sole

This novel sandwich would be great with an Italian Pinot Grigio, such as Toresella 1986. *S.M.*

Halibut

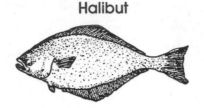

HALIBUT FILLETS WITH MISO SAUCE

Halibut is a sweet-flavored fish, and when prepared in this delicate Japanese sauce the taste is especially delicious.

FISH
1 recipe Basic Marinade (see Index)
3 pounds halibut fillets, cut into 8 serving pieces

SAUCE
½ cup plus 2 tablespoons water
½ cup plus 2 tablespoons mirin
2 tablespoons sugar
¾ cup shiro miso (available in Oriental food stores or by mail; see Appendix)
1 tablespoon Japanese light soy sauce (available in Oriental food stores or by mail; see Appendix)

16 ¼-inch-thick lemon slices
Salt (optional)

1. Marinate the fish: Place the marinade in a large plastic bag. Add the fish and secure the bag with a twister seal. Turn the bag several times, making sure that all fish surfaces touch the marinade. Set the bag in a bowl and let sit at room temperature for 1 hour.

2. Meanwhile, make the sauce: Combine the water, mirin, and sugar and heat to a boil. Reduce the heat to a simmer and cook for 15 minutes. Stir in the miso and soy sauce. Taste for seasoning, adding salt if desired. Let sit in a saucepan at room temperature until ready to serve.

3.   Grill the fish: Place the lemon slices in pairs on the prepared grill. Remove the fillets from the marinade and arrange each fillet on 2 lemon slices. Grill for 6–8 minutes without turning, until the fish has lost its translucence. Carefully remove the fillets from the grill using two spatulas and discard the lemon slices.

4.   While the fish is grilling, reheat the sauce and pour it into a serving bowl. Bring the sauce to the table and spoon liberally over each fillet.

Makes 8 servings (2 cups sauce)

Serving suggestions: rice, pickled ginger slices (available in Oriental food stores or by mail; see Appendix), and Pineapple in Plum Wine (see Index) if serving plum wine with dinner

Fish substitutions: red snapper, mahimahi, yellowtail, scrod

I suggest serving Japanese sake, hot or cold. Or serve a chilled Japanese beer. Japanese plum wine might also be served; it has a sherrylike flavor. *L.S.*

Note: To heat a bottle of sake, bring a pot filled with water to boil. Remove the pot from the heat and place a room-temperature bottle of sake (opened) in the pot. Let stand in hot water for several minutes or until hot. If serving sake chilled, simply pour it into an ice-filled glass. Leftover sake will keep in the refrigerator for about six days after being opened, provided the bottle is well corked or closed. *L.S.*

HALIBUT STEAKS WITH CILANTRO AND LIME BUTTER, GRILLED SHALLOTS AND MUSHROOMS

If you're watching calories, try preparing the lime butter with low-calorie margarine.

LIME BUTTER

1   lime
½   cup (¼ pound) butter or margarine, at room temperature, cut into ½-inch pieces

FISH

3   pounds halibut, cut into 8 steaks
3   cups fresh shiitake mushrooms, trimmed
Melted butter or margarine for brushing fish and vegetables
½   cup minced cilantro
16 large shallots, unpeeled
1   lime, sliced paper-thin, for garnish

1. Make the lime butter: Grate the zest of the lime, place in a bowl, with the juice of the lime. Mix in the butter until combined, using the back of a wooden spoon or a food processor fitted with the steel blade.

2. Brush the halibut steaks and the tops of the mushrooms with melted butter. Sprinkle the fish with cilantro, patting to help the cilantro adhere to the halibut.

3. Grill the vegetables: Put the mushrooms and shallots on the grill. The shallots will take about 8–10 minutes to cook, and the mushrooms will cook quickly, so watch them carefully.

4. Grill the fish: Grill the halibut steaks on the prepared grill for about 6–8 minutes. Turn fish over and continue grilling until done to taste; be sure not to overcook fish.

5.   Place the halibut steaks on a large serving platter and scatter the mushrooms and shallots around the fish. Put a dab of lime butter over each steak and place the lime slices decoratively around the platter.

Makes 8 servings

Serving suggestions: Buckwheat noodles or rice, salad of endive, watercress, and a sprinkle of pine nuts

Fish substitutions: black sea bass, snapper, yellowtail

Good, crisp acidity in the 1986 sauvignon blanc from Frog's Leap makes it a good choice for pairing with the zesty lime butter. *S.M.*

Mackerel

This Atlantic fish has a distinctive flavor and a high fat content. It's similar to the bluefish.

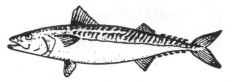

GRILLED DO-IT-YOURSELF SUSHI BAR

Americans are eating more and more sushi—witness the large numbers of sushi bars opening up in our cities. The Chicago area alone boasts several dozen restaurants serving sushi. The word sushi *means "vinegared rice" and refers to a small, bite-sized preparation of rice and fish in combination with other ingredients. But since the fish in sushi is usually—not always, but usually—raw, many people who don't like raw fish are missing out on the fun of this healthful, delicious dish.*

The delicious flavors of sushi can be experienced by raw fish haters with ease. Simply follow our directions for a grilled sushi bar. For those who are scandalized at the thought, relax. We're not breaking completely with tradition. Many of the fish used to make traditional sushi dishes are cooked, including shrimp, crab, and imitation crab.

Here are instructions for setting up your own grilled sushi bar. The type of sushi we're making here is called temaki-sushi, *which means "hand-rolled sushi." Some of the ingredients in our bar may sound odd to you, but once you try them you'll see how delicious they are. These include nori (sheets of pressed seaweed); wasabi paste (horseradish), which comes in tubes; beefstock leaf (a green leaf with a special flavor, grown in California as well as Japan); and pickled ginger. All of these ingredients are available by mail (see the Appendix for a list of sources).*

1⅓ pounds mackerel fillets

3½ cups cooked Sushi Rice (recipe follows)

4 teaspoons wasabi paste or powder (available in Oriental food stores or by mail; see Appendix)

1 package nori (10 8-inch square sheets pressed seaweed, available in Oriental food stores or by mail; see Appendix)

1 pound imitation crab fingers

2 medium-sized avocados

1 large cucumber

1 bowl Japanese soy sauce (*not* the heavier Chinese variety; available in Oriental food stores or by mail; see Appendix)

2-3 ounces red salmon roe

3 ounces pickled ginger (available in Oriental food stores or by mail; see Appendix)

1.   Grill the fish: Arrange the mackerel fillets on the prepared grill. Cook for 4–8 minutes, then turn fillets and continue cooking for 4–8 minutes or until done. Remove from the grill and allow to cool. Place the cooled mackerel on a serving platter and cut into very thin strips.

2.   Transfer the cooled sushi rice to a serving bowl.

3.   Spoon some wasabi paste into a small bowl or place wasabi powder in a bowl and stir a few drops of water into it—just enough to make a paste.

4.   Cut the sheets of nori in half so that each measures 8 inches by 8 inches. Lay them in a stack on a serving plate.

5.   Arrange the crab fingers on a flat serving plate. Then peel the avocados and cut them into thin, 1-inch-long slices and place on a separate serving platter. Peel the cucumber, cut in half lengthwise, remove the seeds, and cut the cucumber into thin matchsticks, ¼ inch wide and 1 inch long. Arrange the cucumber sticks on a separate serving platter. Pour Japanese soy sauce into a small serving bowl.

6.   Spoon the salmon roe into a small bowl and arrange the pickled ginger in another small bowl.

TO ASSEMBLE THE SUSHI BAR

7.   Lay the dishes of ingredients on the table in the following order, so guests may begin at one end and proceed toward the other, adding ingredients to their temaki-sushi as they go: nori, sushi rice, wasabi, mackerel, imitation crab, avocado, cucumber, beefsteak leaf, salmon roe, pickled ginger, soy sauce.

TO MAKE TEMAKI-SUSHI

8.   Pick up a half sheet of nori and hold it in your left hand (assuming you are right-handed). Spoon 2 to 3 tablespoons of rice into the center of the nori and flatten it slightly. Dip a finger into the wasabi paste and run a very thin line of it down the center of the rice; use wasabi paste sparingly, as it is very hot.

9.   Arrange a strip of mackerel or a small piece of imitation crab over the wasabi and rice. Top with a few avocado pieces, a few cucumber matchsticks, a piece of beefsteak leaf, and a sprinkling of salmon roe.

10.   Finally, roll the filled nori slowly and carefully into a cone shape—it should resemble an ice cream cone with a pointed bottom. Twist the bottom of the cone carefully to make certain that it will not leak at the bottom and will stay closed.

11.   Place two or three pieces of pickled ginger on your plate. Then dip your temaki-sushi cone into the bowl of soy sauce. Begin to eat, taking small bites from the wide end of the cone. Eat slices of pickled ginger in between bites.

Makes 20 temaki-sushi, 6–8 servings

Serving suggestions: fresh orange slices, orange sherbert, or Pineapple in Plum Wine (see Index) for dessert

Fish substitutions: grilled yellowtail, shrimp, tuna

Drink Japanese beer, or cold sake over ice cubes, or a light California chardonnay. *S.M.*

SUSHI RICE

1⅛   cups uncooked Japanese rice (available in Oriental food stores or by mail; see Appendix)

1⅛   cups water

⅓   cup Japanese rice vinegar (available in Oriental food stores or by mail; see Appendix)

2   tablespoons sugar

¼   teaspoon salt

1. The night before your sushi party, rinse the rice in a colander, drain, place in a bowl, cover, and refrigerate overnight.

2. Place the rice in a medium saucepan or an electric rice cooker. Stir in the water. Bring to a boil over medium-high heat, and cook for 8–10 minutes. Reduce the heat to a simmer, cover, and cook for 18–20 minutes. Turn off the heat and allow the pan to sit with the cover on for 15 minutes before removing the lid. If using an electric rice cooker, follow the manufacturer's directions.

3. Combine the remaining ingredients in a small pan over medium heat. Cook until the sugar dissolves, stirring occasionally.

4. Working lightly, with a wooden spoon, work the mixture into the rice. Place in a serving bowl and serve immediately.

Makes 3–3½ cups rice

SADA HAKANATA'S SABA NO MISO YAKI (GRILLED MACKEREL IN MISO SAUCE)

This traditional Japanese recipe is based on an ingredient called miso, *which is a fermented soybean paste with a delicate, distinctive flavor. Miso can be ordered by mail through the Star Market (see Appendix). The two basic types of miso are aka miso, which is reddish-colored, and the more delicate shiro miso, which is white and best for fish marinades. Since the different brands of shiro miso on the market vary considerably in sweetness, you may want to add sugar to our recipe below.*

Once your package of miso is opened, simply place any unused portion in a plastic bag and secure with a twister seal. Then set the plastic bag in a jar or container with a lid and store it in the refrigerator. Even after having been opened, it will keep for up to a year.

Although this dish sounds odd, we strongly urge you to try it. It is very simple to prepare; the miso is mixed with brown sugar and mirin, a Japanese cooking wine also available at Japanese markets or by mail order (see Appendix). And it is absolutely delicious. The Japanese often leave the fish in the miso for up to three days or even longer, but for American tastes 24 hours should be sufficient. Although mackerel is particularly delicious when marinated in miso, almost any soft- to medium-firm-fleshed fish, such as red snapper, cod, or even whitefish fillets, can be substituted.

This particular recipe is a gift of Sada Hakanata, one of the owners of the Star Market in Chicago.

FISH
Salt
3 pounds mackerel fillets with skin, cut into 3-inch pieces

MARINADE
4 cups (about 2 pounds) shiro miso (white bean paste, available in Oriental food stores or by mail; see Appendix)

1⅓ cups mirin (Japanese sweet rice wine used for cooking, available in Oriental food stores or by mail; see Appendix)

1 cup brown sugar (more to taste if bean paste is not faintly sweet)
Lemon wedges

1. Salt the mackerel fillets lightly on all sides and allow to stand for 10 minutes.

2. Meanwhile, make the marinade: combine the shiro miso, mirin, and brown sugar in a bowl and taste. It should have a slightly sweet flavor. If it does not, add an additional teaspoon or more of brown sugar.

3. Add the mackerel fillets to the bowl and rub the marinade into the fish on all sides. Transfer the fish and miso to a large plastic bag, roll it up tightly, and wrap the fish-filled bag tightly with plastic wrap. Refrigerate for 24 hours.

4. Grill the fish: At serving time, remove the mackerel from the marinade and use paper towels to wipe some—not all—of the miso off the fillets. Place the fillets skin side down on the prepared grill. Cook for 4–8 minutes or until the skin becomes crisp and black. Immediately turn the mackerel carefully with a spatula or tongs and grill until done to taste. Transfer the mackerel pieces to a serving platter and serve immediately with lemon wedges.

Makes 8 servings

Serving suggestions: rice, green salad, pickled ginger slices (available in Oriental food stores or by mail; see Appendix)

Fish substitutions: whitefish, bluefish, yellowtail

The intense marinade and fishy quality of the mackerel require sake—preferably served hot. *L.S.*

Note: See directions for heating and storing sake in Halibut Fillets with Miso Sauce (see Index).

GRILLED MACKEREL WITH GREEN GRAPES

GRAPE SAUCE

1   16½-ounce can green grapes in light syrup
½   cup water
2   tablespoons sugar
1½ teaspoons cornstarch
1   tablespoon fresh lemon juice
1   tablespoon grated lemon zest

FISH

2   large lemons, each cut into 8 slices
8   10- to 12-ounce mackerel, split, heads removed
Oil for brushing fish
Salt and freshly ground pepper to taste

1.   Make the sauce: Mix the grapes, ¼ cup of the grape juice, and the water in a medium saucepan. Stir in the sugar and cook over medium heat until the grapes are warm but not broken. In a small dish, blend the cornstarch and 1 tablespoon of water. Blend the cornstarch mixture into the sauce and bring to a boil, stirring until the sauce thickens and is clear. Stir in the lemon juice and zest.

2.   Grill the fish: Place 2 lemon slices in each fish cavity; brush the mackerel with oil and sprinkle with salt and pepper. Place on the prepared grill or aluminum foil and cook for about 4–8 minutes. Turn mackerel and grill until done to taste. Transfer the fish to a serving platter and drizzle the hot sauce over the fish.

Makes 8 servings (1½ cups sauce)

Serving suggestions: grilled mushrooms, mixed green salad, fresh raspberries and cream for dessert

Fish substitutions: bluefish, yellowtail

A macon blanc from southern burgundy, such as Les Chazalles Vielle Vignes 1985, made from old vines, would make a wonderful partner for the mackerel and green grapes. *S.M.*

Mahimahi
Mahimahi is a medium-textured fish with a delicate flavor.

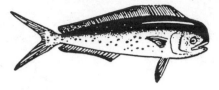

MAHIMAHI SEAFOOD RANCHERO

3–4   4-inch pieces mesquite wood

RANCHERO SALSA
2   tablespoons good-quality olive oil
½   cup minced red onion
3   Anaheim chilies, seeded and chopped
2   cups diced fresh tomato
1   tablespoon fresh lime juice
½   cup minced cilantro
¼   teaspoon salt
2   dashes Tabasco sauce

MARINADE
½   cup good-quality olive oil
1½   cups fresh lime juice
½   teaspoon red pepper flakes
2   large bay leaves

FISH
3   pounds mahimahi, cut into 8 fillets
8   corn tortillas
2   cups shredded cheddar cheese
1   cup chopped scallions

1. Soak the mesquite in cold water to cover for 1 hour.

2. Make the salsa: Heat the oil in a saucepan, add the onion and chilies, and sauté until tender. Add the tomatoes, lime juice, cilantro, salt, and Tabasco. Continue cooking for 1 minute, stirring to combine.

3. Make the marinade: Combine the marinade ingredients, pour into a large plastic bag, and set the bag in a bowl. Add fillets and secure with a twister seal. Turn the bag several times to make sure all fish surfaces touch the marinade. Let sit at room temperature for 1 hour.

4. Grill the fish: Drain the mesquite and place it over the hot coals. Replace the grill and place the mahimahi on the prepared grill. Cook for 4–5 minutes, turn, and continue grilling for about 4 minutes until the fish is cooked to taste. Wrap the tortillas in aluminum foil and warm them on the grill.

5. Lay a warm tortilla on each plate. Ladle salsa over the tortilla and sprinkle with cheese. Arrange grilled mahimahi on top and sprinkle with chopped scallions. Serve hot.

Makes 8 servings (3 cups sauce)

Serving suggestions: Spanish rice, mixed green salad with hearts of palm, grilled Anaheim pepper strips

Fish substitutions: halibut, black sea bass

Sauvignon blanc is a great complement to this spicy dish. *S.M.*

Marlin

Marlin is a meaty fish with a mild flavor. It tastes great marinated.

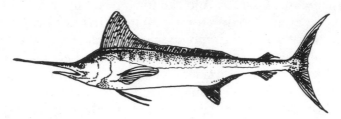

MARLIN WITH BAY LEAVES
AND BASIL BUTTER

FISH

1   recipe Basic Marinade (see Index)
⅓   cup large bay leaves
3   pounds marlin, cut into 8 steaks

BASIL BUTTER

¾   cup (6 ounces) butter or margarine, cut into ½-inch pieces
½   cup trimmed chopped fresh basil

    1.   Marinate the fish: Combine the marinade and bay leaves in a large plastic bag, place the bag in a bowl, add the fish, and secure with a twister seal. Turn the bag several times to make certain all fish surfaces touch the marinade. Let sit at room temperature for 1 hour, turning the bag occasionally.

    2.   Make the basil butter: In a food processor fitted with the steel blade or in a blender, cream the butter with the basil. Place the butter in a bowl and set aside.

    3.   Grill the fish: Remove the marlin from the marinade and place the fish on the prepared grill, making sure some of the bay leaves adhere to the fish. Cook the fish for about 4–8 minutes, turn marlin carefully and cook for 4–5 minutes or until the fish has lost its translucence. Remove the marlin skin, discard bay leaves, and serve fish hot with the soft basil butter.

Makes 8 servings

Serving suggestions: squid ink pasta or other flavored pasta, grilled shrimp salad

Fish substitutions: shark, mahimahi

Fiano di Avelino, produced by the Mastroberardino family in Campania, has a rich, slightly oily texture, similar to that of the marlin. This wine gets better with age—look for the 1980. *S.M.*

Monkfish

Monkfish is also known as "poor man's lobster" because of its lobsterlike texture.

MONKFISH WITH CRACKED GREEN OLIVES

This delicious and unusual combination of sour green olives and fresh fish is popular in Morocco. The olives are brought to a boil three times to rid them of bitterness. Monkfish is at its best here, when its bland flavor and thick, meaty texture is enhanced by the strong garlic marinade and the sour olive topping. Green Greek olives are available at Greek and Middle Eastern markets.

1½ cups drained green Greek olives

MARINADE
¾ cup fresh lemon juice
6 tablespoons imported mild, good-quality olive oil
Large handful parsley, stems removed
6 cloves garlic, peeled and quartered
1½ teaspoons paprika
¾ teaspoon salt
½ teaspoon freshly ground pepper

FISH
3 pounds monkfish, cut into 8 fillets

SAUCE

4 tablespoons butter or margarine
2 tablespoons imported mild, good-quality olive oil
2 medium onions, chopped fine (about 1 cup)
3 cloves garlic, minced fine
1½ large lemons, sliced paper-thin, seeds removed
1 teaspoon ground ginger
1 teaspoon salt
½ teaspoon freshly ground pepper
¼ teaspoon ground cumin
¼–½ cup water (as needed)
⅓–½ cup chopped fresh parsley

16 ¼-inch-thick slices lemon for grilling fillets

1. Put the olives in a single layer within a folded towel and lightly hit the top of the towel with a wooden mallet, hammer, or stone. Then pick out the pits and discard. Or, if desired, pit each olive individually, using a small, sharp knife.

2. Place the olives in a saucepan, cover with water, and heat to a boil. Drain the olives and return to the saucepan. Cover with water and heat again to a boil. Drain and repeat the process a third time, then drain olives again and reserve.

3. Make the marinade: Place the lemon juice, olive oil, parsley, garlic, paprika, salt, and pepper in a blender or a food processor fitted with the steel blade and pulse until the parsley and garlic are finely chopped and the mixture is well combined.

4. Pour the marinade into a large plastic bag and set the bag in a bowl. If the monkfish fillets are very uneven in thickness, butterfly the thick portions so that the fish will cook evenly. Prick the monkfish with fork tines several times, then place the fillets in the bag and secure the bag with a twister seal. Turn the bag several times to make sure all fish surfaces touch the marinade. Let sit at room temperature for 1 hour, turning occasionally.

5.   Meanwhile, make the sauce: Heat the butter and oil in a large, heavy-bottomed frying pan until the butter is melted. Add the onions and garlic and sauté over medium heat for 15 or 20 minutes, until the onions are cooked through.

6.   Add the paper-thin lemon slices, ginger, salt, pepper, and cumin along with ¼ cup of the water and heat to a simmer. Simmer for 15 minutes, stirring occasionally to make sure the mixture does not stick.

7.   Add the parsley, drained olives, and additional water if needed. Heat again to a simmer, cook for a minute, then turn off the heat. The sauce should be thick.

8.   Grill the fish: Remove the monkfish from the marinade. Arrange the ¼-inch-thick lemon slices in pairs on the prepared grill and place each fillet on two lemon slices. Grill for 15 minutes, without turning, or until the fish is completely cooked through. Transfer the fillets to a serving platter, discarding lemon slices.

9.   Meanwhile, heat the olive sauce until hot, adding another ¼ cup water if needed. Remove the lemon slices from the sauce and discard. Transfer the sauce to a serving bowl and bring to the table. Serve each fillet topped with green olive sauce.

Makes 8 servings

Serving suggestions: cracked wheat salad (tabbouleh) and grilled marinated eggplant and green pepper slices

Fish substitution: swordfish

This dish depends on the garlicky marinade. I suggest serving a sauvignon blanc, since it would not be intimidated by the garlic. The really adventure-some might want to try an '86 Beaujolais-Villages, well chilled. Do not serve a red wine. *L.S.*

OCEAN PERCH WITH
PINE NUT BUTTER SAUCE

Pine nuts have such a delicate taste that we've combined them with an equally delicate fish—ocean perch fillets.

PINE NUT BUTTER SAUCE

¾ cup pine nuts
1 cup (½ pound) butter or margarine
4 teaspoons finely chopped chives

FISH

12 ¼-inch-thick slices lemon for grilling
3 pounds ocean perch fillets

1. Toast the pine nuts: Preheat the oven to 350°F. Arrange the pine nuts in a single layer on a baking sheet and toast them in the oven for about 10 minutes, watching carefully. After the first 5 minutes, check every minute or so to make sure they don't burn. As soon as they are lightly browned, remove from the oven.

2. Place the butter in a small saucepan and heat until melted. Add the toasted pine nuts and chives, stir thoroughly, and transfer to a serving bowl.

3. Grill the fish: Arrange the lemon slices on the prepared grill. Place the fillets on the lemon slices and grill for 2–6 minutes without turning, or until they have lost their translucence and are thoroughly cooked.

4. Use two spatulas to remove the fillets carefully from the grill and transfer them to a serving platter. Discard the lemon slices. Serve immediately, topped with pine nut butter sauce.

Makes 8 servings (1½ cups sauce)

Serving suggestions: rice, green salad

Fish substitutions: rockfish, sea trout, orange roughy

The delicate nature of this dish calls for a wine that will not overpower the combined lightness of the sauce and ocean perch. A buttery, lighter chardonnay from California would be delicious. Or, if you wish to serve a French wine, a Mercurey Blanc or a Beaujolais Blanc would be fine. *L.S.*

Ono

Ono, a delicate-flavored fish in the mackerel family, is caught commercially in the Pacific.

ONO GRILLED ON A BED OF TARRAGON LEAVES

1   recipe Basic Marinade (see Index)
3   pounds ono fillets, cut into 8 serving pieces
3   cups fresh tarragon
½   teaspoon fennel seed

    1.   Marinate the fish: Pour the marinade into a large plastic bag, place the bag in a bowl, and add the ono fillets. Secure with a twister seal and turn the bag several times to make sure all fish surfaces touch the marinade. Let sit at room temperature for 1 hour.

    2.   Grill the fish: Arrange a bed of tarragon on the prepared grill. Some of the leaves will fall through the grill onto the hot coals, adding their own special essence to the fish. Place the ono on the tarragon and sprinkle with the fennel. Cook the fish for 4–8 minutes, turn, and continue grilling until the ono is cooked to taste. Serve hot.

Makes 8 servings

Serving suggestions: garlic-basil fettucini, salad of Bibb lettuce and yellow cherry tomatoes

Fish substitutions: swordfish, pompano

The herbaceousness of the tarragon and fennel makes the 1985 Crozes-Hermitage blanc from Jaboulet, a white wine from the northern Rhône, a perfect choice. *S.M.*

Orange Roughy

Orange Roughy is a very mild, delicate fish.

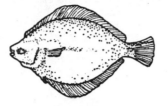

ORANGE ROUGHY WITH BLACK BUTTER SAUCE

FISH

3-4   limes, sliced thin (you'll need 16 slices altogether)
  3   pounds orange roughy fillets, cut into 8 serving pieces
Good-quality olive oil for brushing fish

BLACK BUTTER SAUCE

  1   cup (½ pound) butter
  2   tablespoons red wine vinegar
  4   tablespoons drained capers

1.   Grill the fish: Arrange the lime slices in pairs on the prepared grill. Place one roughy fillet on each pair of limes. Brush the fish with the olive oil. Grill for about 4–6 minutes, without turning, until the fillets have lost their translucence and are slightly browned on the edges.

2.   Make the sauce: Melt the butter in the frying pan over medium heat on the stove or over a hot grill and brown the butter but do not burn.

3.   Drizzle the butter over the fish on a serving platter. Quickly add the vinegar to the pan and reduce the mixture by half over medium heat; this will take about a minute. Drizzle the sauce over the fish and sprinkle with the capers. Serve immediately.

Makes 8 servings

Serving suggestions: grilled mushrooms sprinkled with chives, celery root salad

Fish substitutions: sole, turbot, ocean perch

With this simple preparation, drink a Tavel rosé from the southern Rhône. Jaboulet's was excellent in 1985. *S.M.*

ORANGE ROUGHY WITH PECAN SAUCE

FISH
1   recipe Basic Marinade (see Index)
3   pounds orange roughy fillets, cut into 8 serving pieces

PECAN SAUCE
1¼   cups (10 ounces) butter or margarine
⅓   cup chopped fresh parsley
⅓   cup ground pecans
1   tablespoon fresh lemon juice
2   tablespoons finely chopped green part of scallion
¼   teaspoon freshly grated nutmeg
⅛   teaspoon Tabasco sauce (more to taste)
1¼   cups pecan halves

16   ¼-inch-thick slices lemon for grilling fillets

1. Marinate the fish: Pour the marinade into a large plastic bag and place the bag in a bowl. Add the orange roughy fillets and secure with a twister seal. Turn the bag several times to make certain the marinade touches all fish surfaces. Let sit at room temperature for 1 hour, turning bag occasionally.

2. Make the sauce: Melt the butter in a small frying pan or saucepan. Add the parsley, ground pecans, lemon juice, scallion, nutmeg, and Tabasco. Simmer over low heat for 1 minute. Then add the pecan halves, tossing them well with the butter mixture. Turn off the heat until ready to serve.

3. Grill the fish: Arrange the lemon slices in pairs on the prepared grill, then place each fillet on two lemon slices. Grill for 4–6 minutes, without turning, or until the fish is cooked through and has lost its translucence. Transfer the fillets carefully to a serving platter and discard the lemon slices.

4. Reheat the sauce, transfer it to a serving bowl, and serve each fillet topped with pecan sauce.

Makes 8 servings (1⅔ cups sauce)

Serving suggestions: tart green salad, rice, fruit for dessert

Fish substitutions: catfish, scrod, halibut

Because of the nutty butter sauce, a fruity wine (one that has a taste of the grape without being overly sweet) would be ideal. A German Rhine or Moselle, particularly one made from the Riesling grape, would be a good match. *L.S.*

ORANGE ROUGHY WITH CHAMPAGNE SAUCE

CHAMPAGNE SAUCE
2 tablespoons butter or margarine
1 tablespoon flour
1 cup dry Champagne
1¼ cups whipped cream
½ teaspoon dried basil, crumbled
½ teaspoon minced fresh parsley
Salt and freshly ground white pepper to taste

FRIED LEEKS
2 cups peanut oil
2 cups finely julienned leeks
Salt to taste

FISH
3 oranges, sliced thin (you'll need 16 slices for grilling; use any remaining slices for garnish)
3 pounds orange roughy fillets, cut into 8 serving pieces
3 tablespoons dried basil, crumbled

1. Make the sauce: melt the butter in a medium saucepan and whisk in the flour. Stir in the Champagne. Continue cooking over medium heat until the liquid is reduced by half. Stir in the cream, basil, parsley, and salt and pepper. Cook over medium-low heat until the sauce thickens slightly. Taste and adjust seasonings.

2. Fry the leeks: Heat the oil to 375°F in a large, heavy skillet. Pat the leeks dry with paper toweling and slide into the oil. The leeks will brown quickly. Remove with a slotted spoon almost immediately and drain on paper toweling. Reserve for garnish.

3. Grill the fish: Arrange 16 of the orange slices in pairs on the prepared grill. Place one fillet on each pair of orange slices and sprinkle with basil. Grill for 4–6 minutes, without turning, or until the fillets have lost their translucence and are slightly browned on the edges.

4.   When the fillets are cooked, transfer them to a serving platter and garnish the platter with fried leeks and any remaining orange slices. Serve with the warm Champagne sauce.

Makes 8 servings (1¾ cups sauce)

Serving suggestions: Waldorf salad, clusters of grapes, hot French bread

Fish substitutions: sole, flounder, ocean perch

A full-bodied, toasty champagne, such as Veuve Clicquot Brut non vintage, makes this a festive dish. *S.M.*

ROUGHY BURRITOS

BURRITO SALSA

4 large tomatoes
2 fresh or canned jalapeño peppers, seeded and chopped fine
2 cloves garlic, minced
5 scallions, minced
½ cup chopped cilantro
¼ teaspoon salt
⅛ teaspoon freshly ground pepper

FISH

1¾ pounds orange roughy fillets
Oil for brushing fish
1 teaspoon pure chili powder
1 teaspoon ground cumin
2 green bell peppers, cored, seeded, and sliced into thin rings
½ cup chopped pitted black olives
8 10-inch flour tortillas
2 8-ounce cans green chilies, drained
2-2½ cups shredded Monterey Jack cheese
3 fresh or canned jalapeño peppers, seeded and chopped fine

1. Make the salsa: Blanch the tomatoes in boiling water for 45 seconds or until the skins are loose. Remove and discard skins. Chop the tomatoes and put in a bowl with the jalapeños. Add the garlic, scallions, cilantro, salt, and pepper. Taste and adjust seasonings. Let the salsa stand for 1 hour before serving.

2. Grill the fish: Brush the fish with oil and sprinkle with chili powder and cumin. Grill for about 4-6 minutes, without turning, on slices of green pepper on the prepared grill, until the fillets have lost their translucence or until done to taste. Break the fish into chunks and place in a bowl with the pepper rings. Sprinkle with olives.

3. Wrap the tortillas in aluminum foil. Heat the tortillas on the grill until warm and wrap in a cloth napkin. Put the green chilies, jalapeños, and

shredded cheese into three bowls. Toss the salsa ingredients in the bowl. Arrange the grilled roughy, green chilies, jalapeños, cheese, and salsa on the table.

4.   Show guests how to assemble a burrito by laying the tortilla flat in front of you on a plate. Place about ⅓ cup of the grilled roughy in the center of the tortilla and sprinkle with green chilies, jalapeños, and cheese to taste. Ladle on a small amount of salsa and roll up the tortilla, folding in one end so that guests can eat the burrito starting at the open end.

Makes 8 burritos (about 2½ cups salsa)

Serving suggestions: refried beans (see Index), corn chips, cold fruit

Fish substitutions: flounder, sole

Since the chilies predominate in this dish, a hearty red, such as a zinfandel from Ridge—the Paso Robles 1985 is rich and spicy—works especially well. *S.M.*

Pompano

Pompano is a relatively small fish, averaging about 2 pounds, and is found in waters from Massachusetts to South America.

POMPANO WITH LIGHT RAISIN SAUCE

LIGHT RAISIN SAUCE

1¼ cups golden raisins
⅓ cup brandy
2 teaspoons minced shallots
1 cup (½ pound) butter or margarine, at room temperature
1 cup dry white wine
½ cup heavy cream
Salt and freshly ground white pepper to taste

FISH

4 tablespoons butter or margarine at room temperature
2 tablespoons grated lemon zest
2 tablespoons minced fresh parsley
3 pounds pompano fillets, cut into 8 serving pieces

1.   Make the sauce: Soak the raisins in the brandy in a small bowl for 45 minutes; drain.
2.   Sauté the shallots in 2 tablespoons of the butter for 1 minute. Stir in the wine. Cook over medium-high heat until the mixture is reduced to 4–5 tablespoons of liquid. Strain and return the liquid to the pan. Blend in the cream and heat until warm. Remove from the heat. Whisk in the remaining butter, about 2–3 tablespoons at a time. Mix in the raisins. Set aside.

3. Grill the fish: Soften the butter in a bowl with a wooden spoon. Blend in the lemon zest and parsley. Spread the butter mixture over the fish. Place the fish on the prepared grill and cook for about **3–5** minutes. Turn over and grill until done to taste or finish cooking without turning. Transfer the fish to a serving platter and drizzle the warm sauce over the fish.

Makes 8 servings (3 cups sauce)

Serving suggestions: cucumber salad, mixed grilled vegetables, whole-wheat bread or rolls

Fish substitutions: ono, mackerel, yellowtail

Vouvray, made from chenin blanc grapes in the Loire, is off-dry, complementing the slightly sweet raisin sauce. Try Chapin-Landais 1986. *S.M.*

Red Snapper

Red Snapper is a favorite fish for entertaining. It's a medium-firm fish with a mild flavor.

RED SNAPPER FILLETS WITH GORGONZOLA

2   tablespoons plus 2 teaspoons cashews
1   pound Gorgonzola cheese or any good-quality blue cheese at room temperature
¼   cup farmer cheese, at room temperature
¼   cup cream cheese, at room temperature
3   pounds red snapper fillets, cut into 8 serving pieces
16   ¼-inch-thick lemon slices for grilling

1.   Toast the cashews: Place the nuts in a single layer in a frying pan and set over medium heat. Watch carefully, stirring often. As soon as the nuts begin to brown, stir constantly for about 1 minute, until lightly browned on all sides. Remove from heat and allow to cool, then chop the nuts.

2.   Combine the Gorgonzola, farmer cheese, cream cheese, and chopped cashews in a small bowl. Spread and pat the mixture over the tops of the fillets to cover.

3.   Grill the fish: Place the lemon slices on the prepared grill. Arrange the fillets, Gorgonzola side up, on the lemon slices. Grill for 4–8 minutes, without turning, or until the fillets are cooked through and have lost their translucence.

4.   Use two spatulas to carefully remove the fillets from the grill and transfer them to a serving platter. Discard the lemon slices and serve the fish immediately.

Makes 8 servings (2¼ cups spread)

Serving suggestions: tart green salad, steamed small new potatoes tossed with a minimal amount of butter or margarine

Fish substitution: black sea bass

With this fish recipe, you can forget the cautionary "no red wine with fish." A light Gamay Beaujolais from California or a young bordeaux supérieur would enhance the flavors of the blue cheese and snapper. *L.S.*

CHINESE CABBAGE PACKETS

For a less charred effect you can wrap the fish packets in aluminum foil; seal tightly before grilling.

FILLING
3 tablespoons peanut oil
3 scallions, minced
½ teaspoon ground ginger
½ teaspoon garlic powder
2 cups bean sprouts, rinsed with hot water and drained
½ cup chopped water chestnuts
½ teaspoon soy sauce
½ teaspoon Oriental sesame oil
¼ teaspoon salt
⅛ teaspoon freshly ground pepper

FISH
24 large leaves (about 1 large head) Chinese cabbage
2¼ pounds red snapper fillets, cut into 12 equal pieces
12 small snow peas, strings removed, trimmed
Oil for brushing packets

1. Make the filling: Heat the oil in a wok or heavy skillet; add the scallions, ginger, garlic powder, bean sprouts, and water chestnuts. Stir-fry for 2–3 minutes. Stir in the soy sauce, sesame oil, salt, and pepper. Remove from the heat.

2. Make the packets: Remove the tough end of the cabbage leaves and discard. Blanch cabbage leaves until almost cooked; drain and pat dry. Lay on paper toweling.

3. Put a piece of red snapper in the center of each leaf. Place 2 tablespoons of the filling over the fish. Place 1 snow pea on top. Bring the top of the leaf down to cover the fish, then bring the bottom of the leaf up over the fish, envelope style. Place the packet on a second leaf in the opposite direction so that the exposed sides will be covered. Again bring the top of the cabbage down to the center and the bottom half up over the center. Turn

the packet over, seal side down, on a tray. Brush lightly with oil. Repeat with the remaining ingredients; you should end up with 12 packets.

4. Grill the packets: Place the packets on the prepared grill (coals should be medium-hot) or in a prepared grill basket and grill for 4 minutes. Turn and continue grilling for 2–3 minutes or until done. If the outer leaf is too charred for your taste, you can remove it before serving, leaving the inner leaf in place. Serve hot.

Makes 6 servings (2 packets per person)

Serving suggestions: fried rice or Oriental noodles

Fish substitutions: grouper, black sea bass, striped sea bass

Spicy Oriental dishes are often best complemented by strange and wonderful Alsatian gewürztraminers. With this dish try a Boeckel Reserve 1985. *S.M.*

RED SNAPPER WITH SPANISH WINE BUTTER AND BLACK OLIVE AIOLI

BLACK OLIVE AIOLI

2 tablespoons fine white bread crumbs
½ teaspoon fresh lemon juice
2 large cloves garlic, crushed
1 cup drained pitted black olives
¼ teaspoon salt
2 egg yolks
1 cup good-quality olive oil

SPANISH WINE BUTTER

¾ cup Spanish red wine
1 onion, minced
¾ cup (6 ounces) butter or margarine, at room temperature, cut into 1-inch pieces
1 tablespoon fresh lemon juice
¼ teaspoon salt

FISH

2 large red onions, sliced thin
Good-quality olive oil for brushing onions and fillets
8 8- to 12-ounce red snappers, cleaned, heads removed, or red snapper fillets

    1. Make the black olive aioli: Puree the bread crumbs, lemon juice, and garlic in a food processor fitted with the steel blade or a blender. Add the olives, salt, and egg yolks and process again. With the machine running, pour in the olive oil in a *slow*, steady stream until a sauce is formed. Cover and chill until ready to serve.

    2. Make the wine butter: Simmer the wine with the onion in a medium saucepan until the liquid is reduced to 3–4 tablespoons. Strain. With a wooden spoon, beat in the butter, a small chunk at a time. Season with lemon juice and salt. Cover and serve soft, at room temperature.

3. Grill the fish: Brush the red onion slices with the oil. Arrange the onion slices on the prepared grill and cook for about 3 minutes on each side. Then place the oiled snappers on the grill and cook for about 5–8 minutes. Turn and continue cooking until the fillets are cooked through and have lost their translucence. Or you can grill snapper fillets on the onion slices, without turning.

4. Serve with the wine butter and black olive aioli as a side relish.

Makes 8 servings (1½ cups aioli and 1½ cups wine butter)

Serving suggestions: saffron rice, grilled pepper strips, flan for dessert

Fish substitutions: black sea bass, mullet, pollack

Made from the tempranillo grape, the hearty Monticillo 1980 provides the complexity necessary to complement the simple flavors of garlic, olives, and onions. *S.M.*

GRILLED RED SNAPPER ALFREDO

FISH
Basic marinade (see Index)
2   pounds red snapper fillets

ALFREDO SAUCE
2   cups whipping cream
⅓   pound Parmesan cheese, grated
2   tablespoons butter or margarine
¼   teaspoon freshly grated nutmeg

PASTA
1   pound fettuccine, cooked according to package directions
⅓   cup freshly grated Parmesan cheese

1.   Marinate the fish: Pour the marinade into a large plastic bag and add the snapper fillets. Secure the bag with a twister seal and turn the bag several times to make sure all fish surfaces touch the marinade. Place the bag in a bowl and let sit at room temperature for 1 hour.

2.   While the red snapper is marinating, make the sauce: Heat the cream in the top of a double boiler over simmering water until the cream is hot. Stir in the cheese slowly, whisking until blended. Whisk in the butter. Remove the pan from the heat. Continue beating until the sauce thickens. Season with nutmeg.

3.   Grill the fish: Arrange the fish on the prepared grill and cook for 4–8 minutes. Turn the fish and continue grilling until done to taste.

4.   Warm the sauce over low heat about 2 minutes before serving.

5.   Transfer the fish to a plate and break it into small irregular pieces using two forks.

6.   Refresh the fettuccine under hot water in a colander. Toss the warm noodles with the Alfredo sauce and fish chunks. Serve immediately.

Makes 8–10 servings (2¼–2⅓ cups sauce)

Serving suggestions: endive salad or mixed green salad, warm Italian bread

Fish substitutions: rockfish, swordfish

The richness of the Alfredo sauce needs a great balance between flavor and "cut"—try the chardonnay from Lungarotti, a well-respected producer from Umbria. *S.M.*

RED SNAPPER WITH MARZIPAN

This crowd-stopping dish is known as hut b'noua *in the Moroccan fishing city of Safi, where it originated. The unlikely combination of orange-flavored almond paste and fresh fish is superb; your guests will be astonished when they taste it and will beg for the recipe. The original dish is made with a large whole red snapper that is gutted and scaled, filled with orange-flavored almond paste, and topped with more paste. The fish is then oven-baked on a bed of chopped onions. Our version is made with snapper fillets that are spread with an almond paste topping and grilled. We do not suggest that you try to grill this dish the traditional way, using a whole fish, because half-cooked large fish fall apart on the grill when they are turned. We like this dish better using fillets, in any case, because it is so refined in flavor and concept that no one should have to deal with the indignity of fish bones. In the original recipe, the almond paste was flavored with cinnamon and orange flower water, but we have substituted grated orange zest and orange juice. When you make the almond paste, keep it fairly dry. If it is limp, too much of it will run off the fillet during grilling.*

FISH
½   cup imported mild, good-quality olive oil
3   tablespoons fresh lemon juice
3   pounds red snapper fillets, cut into 8 serving pieces

ALMOND PASTE
1½   cups blanched almonds
1   scant cup sugar
Zest from ½ large orange, removed with vegetable peeler and diced coarse
3   tablespoons fresh orange juice
2   tablespoons salad oil

Salt and freshly ground pepper to taste
16   ¼-inch thick orange or onion slices, for grilling fish

    1.   Marinate the fish: Mix the olive oil and lemon juice and pour into a large plastic bag. Set the bag in a bowl and add the fish fillets. Secure the bag with a twister seal and turn the bag a few times to make certain all fish surfaces touch the marinade. Let sit at room temperature for 1 hour.

2.   Meanwhile, make the almond paste: Preheat the oven to 350°F. Place the almonds in a single layer on a baking sheet and place in the oven for 8–10 minutes, watching carefully. Check every couple of minutes after the first 3–4 minutes and remove the almonds when lightly toasted.

3.   Transfer the toasted almonds to a blender or food processor fitted with the steel blade. Add the sugar, orange zest, orange juice, and salad oil. Process the mixture by pulsing and checking the consistency until a coarse paste results.

4.   Arrange the fillets, skin side down, on a platter. Salt and pepper each fillet liberally, then use paper towels to pat the top of each fillet dry. Top each with a scant ¼ cup almond paste, spreading it as evenly as possible.

5.   Grill the fish: Lay the orange or onion slices in pairs on the prepared grill. Arrange the fillets on top of the orange or onion slices. Grill without turning until the fillets are cooked through, watching carefully.

6.   Using two spatulas, carefully transfer the fillets from the grill to a serving platter. Discard the orange or onion slices. Serve immediately.

Makes 8 servings (2 cups almond paste)

Serving suggestions: tart green salad, hot French bread

Fish substitutions: scrod, halibut

This sweet dish calls for a wine that will function in a subtle way as an undertone. I suggest serving a Johannisberg Riesling of medium sweetness or a sweeter Vouvray. *L.S.*

RED SNAPPER NEW ORLEANS–STYLE

NEW ORLEANS–STYLE SAUCE

4   tablespoons good-quality olive oil
3   cloves garlic, minced
1   medium-large onion, minced
2   cups chopped peeled tomatoes
1   teaspoon paprika
½   teaspoon dried thyme, crushed
2   large bay leaves
⅛   teaspoon freshly ground pepper
⅛   teaspoon red pepper flakes, crushed
1   teaspoon prepared mustard

FISH

8   8 to 10-ounce red snappers, scaled and cleaned, heads and tails left on
Olive oil for brushing fish
8   slices lemon or lime
½   cup crumbled bay leaves

1.   Make the sauce: Heat the oil in a medium pan; add the garlic and onion and sauté until tender. Add the remaining sauce ingredients and sauté for 2 minutes, stirring often. Discard the bay leaves.

2.   Grill the fish: Brush fish with oil and place a lemon or lime slice in each fish cavity. Sprinkle the bay leaves over the hot coals. Place the fish on the prepared grill and cook for 4–8 minutes. Turn fish over carefully with a long-handled spatula and continue to grill until done to taste. Reheat the sauce while the fish is cooking.

4.   Serve the fish hot, topped with the hot New Orleans–style sauce.

Makes 8 servings (1¾–2¼ cups sauce)

Serving suggestions: three-bean salad or garbanzo bean salad, grilled scallions, grilled large garlic cloves, hot French bread

Fish substitutions: sea bass, ocean perch, halibut steaks

A sauvignon blanc, such as Clos du Bois barrel-fermented 1986, with its crisp acidity and a touch of wood, makes a great complement to the grill flavor and tangy sauce. *S.M.*

RED SNAPPER WITH PINEAPPLE SALSA

Pineapple adds a new twist to an old southwestern treat. You may want to prepare extra to pass at the table.

2   cups mesquite chips

PINEAPPLE SALSA
½   cup minced cilantro
1   green bell pepper, seeded and minced
1   yellow bell pepper, seeded and minced
1   medium-large onion, minced
2   cups minced fresh pineapple

FISH
⅓   cup peanut oil
Juice of 3 limes
3   pounds red snapper fillets, cut into 8 serving pieces

1.   Soak the mesquite chips in cold water to cover for 1 hour.
2.   Make the salsa: Toss the cilantro, peppers, onion, and pineapple in a mixing bowl. Cover and chill until ready to serve.
3.   Grill the fish: Drain the mesquite chips and scatter them over the hot coals; replace the grill. Combine the oil and fresh lime juice and baste the red snapper with the mixture. Grill the snapper on the prepared grill for about 4–8 minutes. Turn the snapper using a long-handled spatula and continue grilling for 4–8 minutes, or until fish begins to flake when tested with a fork. Place the fish on individual plates and spoon the salsa over the middle section of the fish.

Makes 8 servings (3¼ cups salsa)

Serving suggestions: Refried Beans (see Index) with Spanish rice or grilled corn with a strip of bacon wrapped around it

Fish substitution: black sea bass

Tropical fruit flavors jump from the glass of Kendall-Jackson Vintner's Reserve Chardonnay 1986, making it an excellent partner for the pineapple salsa. *S.M.*

Rockfish
This West Coast fish is medium-firm with a mild flavor.

ROCKFISH WITH WHITE WINE SAUCE

WHITE WINE SAUCE
- 3 tablespoons butter or margarine
- 5 shallots, minced
- ½ cup dry white wine
- 1½ cups half-and-half
- ½ teaspoon dried tarragon, crumbled
- ½ teaspoon dried chervil, crumbled
- ½ teaspoon salt

FISH
- 3 pounds rockfish fillets, cut into 8 serving pieces
- Good-quality olive oil for brushing fish
- 1 bunch chives, trimmed

1.   Make the sauce: Melt the butter in a saucepan; add the shallots and sauté until tender. Add the wine and cook over medium-high heat until reduced to about 5–6 tablespoons of liquid. Strain and return the liquid to the pan. Blend in the half-and-half and season with tarragon, chervil, and salt. Simmer until the sauce is warm, stirring often. Set aside and serve warm.

2.   Grill the fish: Brush the fish with the oil and arrange on the prepared grill. Grill the fish for about 3–5 minutes, turn carefully, and continue grilling until the fish begins to flake when tested with a fork.

3. Serve the fish hot on individual dishes with the white wine sauce. Garnish with chive strips.

Makes 8 servings (1¾ cups sauce)

Serving suggestions: tossed green salad topped with a slice of warm goat cheese, grilled asparagus

Fish substitutions: rainbow trout, flounder

Drink a local white made from the sauvignon blanc grape. The 1986 Pouilly Fumé from Ladoucette is considered a classic. *S.M.*

ROCKFISH FILLETS WITH SAFFRON BEURRE BLANC

SAFFRON BEURRE BLANC
2　large shallots, chopped
1　cup dry white wine
1　cup (½ pound) butter or margarine at room temperature
3　pinches saffron threads soaked in 2 teaspoons hot water
Salt and freshly ground pepper to taste

FISH
3　pounds rockfish fillets, cut into 8 serving pieces
Melted butter or margarine for brushing fish
½　cup minced hazelnuts

1.　Make the sauce: Heat the shallots with the wine in a saucepan, bringing the mixture to a boil over medium heat. Continue cooking until all but 5–6 tablespoons of liquid remain. Strain and return the liquid to the pan. Beat in the butter, about 2 tablespoons at a time, until all the butter has been added. Whisk in the saffron liquid. Season with salt and pepper.

2.　Grill the fish: Brush the fillets with butter and press ¼ cup of the hazelnuts firmly into the fish. Cook on the prepared grill or in a grill basket for 3 minutes. Turn and continue grilling for about 3–5 minutes, until done to taste.

3.　Spoon some of the warm sauce onto each plate, arrange a fish fillet over the sauce, and sprinkle with the remaining hazelnuts. Serve hot.

Makes 8 servings

Serving suggestions: green salad with arugula, French green beans

Fish substitutions: red snapper, black sea bass

Beurre blanc normally requires a more delicate wine, but the addition of saffron calls for something richer. Try the Deloach Chardonnay OFS 1985.
S.M.

Salmon

Salmon is a universal fish, found in both the Atlantic and Pacific Ocean as well as in many lakes. It is a gourmet food that has an ancient history and continues today as a prized delicacy.

STUFFED SALMON WITH WILD MUSHROOMS

WILD MUSHROOM STUFFING
4   tablespoons butter or margarine
1   large onion, minced
2   cups fresh shiitake mushrooms, trimmed
1   cup fresh oyster mushrooms, trimmed and chopped coarse
½   cup bread crumbs
1   carrot, grated
½   teaspoon dried dill
½   teaspoon dried tarragon, crumbled
¼   teaspoon salt
⅛   teaspoon freshly ground pepper

FISH
8   8- to 10-ounce salmon, cleaned and scaled, heads and tails left on
Good-quality olive oil
½   cup drained capers, for garnish

1.   Make the stuffing: Melt the butter in a skillet, add the onion, and sauté about 2 minutes. Stir in the mushrooms and continue cooking until the mushrooms are soft. Toss with the bread crumbs, carrot, dill, tarragon, salt, and pepper.

2. Lightly stuff the salmon, using about 3–5 tablespoons of stuffing per salmon. Brush the salmon with olive oil.

3. Grill the fish: Arrange the salmon on the prepared grill and cook for 4–8 minutes on each side or until it begins to flake easily when tested with a fork.

4. Place one salmon on each plate and garnish with the capers.

Makes 8 servings

Serving suggestions: mixed green salad, warm blueberry muffins

Fish substitutions: trout, whitefish

A lean Oregon Pinot Noir, such as Adelsheim 1984, provides a woodsy complement to the mushrooms as well as a little "bite" to cut the richness of the salmon. *S.M.*

GRILLED SALMON WITH CORN RELISH

This recipe comes from chef Maggie Wanglin.

FISH
4   5-inch skewers
4   5-ounce center-cut skinless salmon fillets, cut in half, each half approximately 1½ inches by 5 inches, for a total of 8 pieces
4   strips bacon
Good-quality olive oil

RELISH
4   strips bacon
1   cup fresh corn kernels
1   red bell pepper, seeded and diced
1   bunch chives, trimmed and minced

1. Soak the skewers in water for 1 hour and drain.
2. Grill the fish: With the thick ends opposite each other, interlock two c-shaped fillets (ying/yang style) into a medallion. Wrap each medallion with a strip of bacon and secure with a skewer. Brush lightly with olive oil and cook on the prepared grill for 3–4 minutes on each side; the centers will be slightly translucent.
3. Make the relish: Sauté bacon until crisp and drain it, discarding all but 1 tablespoon of the drippings. Let the bacon cool and crumble it. Sauté the corn in the tablespoon of bacon drippings. Add red pepper, chives, and crumbled bacon. Place in a small bowl and serve with the salmon.

Makes 4 servings (1½ cups relish)

Serving suggestions: cornbread, tossed green salad

Fish substitutions: salmon, whitefish

Meursault Sous La Velle, Michelot Bulsson 1985, is a rich, buttery, slightly smoky wine complementing the slightly smoky flavor imparted by the bacon.
S.M.

SALMON PATTIES ON THE GRILL

2 tablespoons butter or margarine
½ cup very finely chopped onions
1½ cups toasted bread crumbs
¼ cup evaporated milk
2 eggs, lightly beaten
2–3 tablespoons drained capers
2 tablespoons fresh lemon juice
1 teaspoon salt
½ teaspoon freshly ground pepper
⅛ teaspoon Tabasco sauce (to taste)
2 7¾-ounce cans salmon, drained
2 scallions, green part only
Melted butter or margarine for brushing patties
Dijon mustard

1. Melt the butter in a small saucepan. Add the onion and sauté for 10 minutes over low heat or until the onion is limp and translucent. Transfer to a mixing bowl and add the bread crumbs, evaporated milk, eggs, capers, lemon juice, salt, pepper, and Tabasco sauce.

2. Place the drained salmon in a strainer and press with the back of a wooden spoon to remove as much excess liquid as possible. Add the salmon to the onion/bread crumb mixture. Use scissors to snip the scallions into the mixture, cutting them into small pieces. Mix well, then measure. You should have 3 cups.

3. Measure out a slightly heaping ⅓ cup of the mixture and form into a 4-inch-long oval patty. Repeat with the remaining mixture until you have eight patties.

4. Carefully transfer the patties to the prepared grill and brush with melted butter. Cook for 5 minutes on each side, using a spatula to turn the patties and brushing again with melted butter. Serve immediately with Dijon mustard.

Makes 8 servings

Serving suggestions: french-fried potatoes, hearty coleslaw

Fish substitutions: any other kind of canned salmon; do not substitute canned mackerel or tuna

These salmon patties, raised to haute cuisine status, should be served with a chilled white zinfandel. *L.S.*

Scrod

Scrod is a small cod, a lean fish with firm white meat. It is found in the Atlantic Ocean off Newfoundland south to Massachusetts. I spent my early years in Boston, and I remember fondly this jingle:

"Boston, the home of beans and the Cod,
Where the Lowells talk only to Cabots,
And the Cabots talk only to God."

B.G.

SCROD WITH ANISE BUTTER

ANISE BUTTER
1   teaspoon crushed aniseed
½   cup (¼ pound) butter or margarine, at room temperature
1   tablespoon chopped chives

FISH
Melted butter or margarine for brushing fish
3   pounds scrod fillets, cut into 8 serving pieces

    1.   Make the anise butter: Blend aniseed and butter in a food processor fitted with the steel blade or in a blender. Add the chives and combine.

    2.   Mound the butter in a small bowl, cover, and refrigerate. Remove from refrigerator 45 minutes before serving time so that the butter will be soft when served.

3. Grill the fish: Brush the fish with melted butter. Grill the scrod for 3–6 minutes. Turn and grill 2–3 minutes or until the fish is cooked to taste. Place the fillets on individual plates.

Makes 8 servings

Serving suggestions: mixed green salad, pumpernickel rolls, and grilled mushrooms

Fish substitutions: flounder, cod

Rich and flowery, the white Châteauneuf-du-Pape from Beaucastel, 1985, marries well with the slightly medicinal anise scent. *S.M.*

SCROD FILLETS WITH APRICOT SAUCE

This Persian dish combines apricots, sugar, onions, and pomegranate seeds to form a colorful, unusual jamlike sauce with onion undertones.

FISH

½ cup imported mild, good-quality olive oil
3 tablespoons fresh lemon juice
3 pounds scrod or red snapper fillets, cut into 8 serving pieces
Salt and freshly ground pepper to taste

APRICOT SAUCE

4 tablespoons butter or margarine
6 ounces dried apricots, quartered (about 36)
⅔ cup finely chopped onion (5 ounces)
1 heaping cup fresh pomegranate seeds
6 tablespoons fresh lemon juice
½ cup sugar
¼ teaspoon salt
1½ cups water (more if needed)
16 ¼-inch-thick slices lemon or onion for grilling

    1.   Marinate the fish: Combine the olive oil and 3 tablespoons of the lemon juice in a large plastic bag and place the bag in a bowl. Place the fillets in the bag, secure with a twister seal, and turn the bag several times to make certain all fish surfaces touch the marinade. Let sit at room temperature for 1 hour.

    2.   Make the sauce: Melt 2 tablespoons of the butter in a medium frying pan, add the quartered apricots and sauté for 2–3 minutes. Transfer to a blender or a food processor fitted with the steel blade and process until coarsely chopped.

    3.   Melt the remaining 2 tablespoons butter in the same frying pan, add the onion, and sauté for 10 minutes or until the onion is very limp. Add the pomegranate seeds and cook for an additional minute. Then add the

coarsely chopped apricots, the remaining 6 tablespoons lemon juice, sugar, salt, and water. Stir to combine. Heat to a boil, reduce the heat, and simmer for 15 minutes or until a thick but still liquid sauce results. Add more water if needed.

4.   Grill the fish: Remove the fillets from the marinade. Lightly salt and pepper them on each side. Arrange the lemon or onion slices in pairs on the prepared grill. Then place the fillets on the lemon or onion slices. Grill the fillets for about 3-6 minutes, without turning, until the fillets are completely cooked through and have lost their translucence.

5.   Use two spatulas to transfer each fillet carefully to a serving platter, discarding the onion or lemon slices. Serve immediately, spooning the hot apricot sauce over each fillet.

Makes 8 servings (3 cups sauce)

Serving suggestions: cold rice salad or cracked wheat salad (tabbouleh), hot French bread

Fish substitutions: halibut, ono

Since this dish should not be served with a red wine, choose a Johannisberg Riesling from California or Germany, a chardonnay from California, or a Vouvray, a Loire wine from France. *L.S.*

SCROD FILLETS WITH POMEGRANATE SAUCE

This unusual and delicious sweet-sour Persian sauce is dark brown because of its walnut base. The sauce is flavored with pomegranate syrup. Do not substitute grenadine for pomegranate syrup; grenadine used to be based on real pomegranates, but today it is usually made with artificial flavorings. If you cannot find the syrup, you can substitute pomegranate paste, but you must first thin it with water: mix 6 tablespoons pomegranate paste with 4 tablespoons water; use the resulting 10 tablespoons as pomegranate syrup.

FISH

½	cup imported mild, good-quality olive oil
3	tablespoons fresh lemon juice
3	pounds scrod or red snapper fillets, cut into 8 serving pieces

POMEGRANATE SAUCE

10	ounces (2½ cups) finely ground walnuts
1½	cups water
5–10	tablespoons pomegranate syrup (to taste)
3	tablespoons sugar
¼	teaspoon salt
¼	teaspoon ground cinnamon
¼	teaspoon freshly grated nutmeg
¼	teaspoon freshly ground pepper
1½	teaspoons fresh lemon juice

16	¼-inch-thick slices lemon or orange for grilling

Pomegranate seeds for garnish

1. Marinate the fish: Combine the olive oil and lemon juice in a large plastic bag and place the bag in a bowl. Place the scrod fillets in the bag, secure the bag with a twister seal, and turn the bag several times to make sure all fish surfaces touch the marinade. Let sit at room temperature for 1 hour.

2.   Meanwhile, make the sauce: Combine the ground walnuts, water, and 5 tablespoons of the pomegranate syrup in a medium saucepan, heat to a boil, reduce the heat, and simmer over low heat for 5 minutes. Stir in the sugar, salt, cinnamon, nutmeg, black pepper, and lemon juice. Return to a simmer and cook 15 minutes. Now taste; if the dish is too sweet, and you want more of the faintly sour, pomegranate flavor, add pomegranate syrup, a tablespoon at a time, until you are satisfied with the sweet-and-sour quality. (We usually add 7 or 8 tablespoons of the syrup.)

3.   Grill the fish: Remove the fillets from the marinade. Lay the lemon or orange slices in pairs on the prepared grill. Arrange a fillet on each pair of 2 lemon or orange slices and cook the fillets for about 3–6 minutes, without turning, until the flesh has lost its translucence and is completely cooked.

4.   Using two spatulas, carefully transfer the fillets, one at a time, to a serving platter. Serve a fillet to each guest, spooning warm pomegranate sauce over each. Garnish each serving with a spoonful of fresh pomegranate seeds.

Makes 8 servings (3 cups sauce)

Serving suggestions: rice, grilled vegetables

Fish substitutions: ono, halibut

See the wine suggestions for Scrod Fillets with Apricot Sauce (see Index). *L.S.*

Sea Bass

Sea bass has a delicate flavor and a firm white meat. It is caught in Atlantic waters from New York to North Carolina.

ORIENTAL-STYLE SEA BASS

MARINADE
4   tablespoons light soy sauce
5   tablespoons light brown sugar
1   tablespoon Oriental sesame oil
5   tablespoons fresh lime juice
3   cloves garlic, minced
3   quarter-sized slices fresh gingerroot, minced
¾   teaspoon red pepper flakes

FISH
8   8-ounce sea bass, scaled and cleaned, with heads and tails left on
2   limes, each cut into 8 slices
Peanut oil for greasing grill
1   bunch scallions, trimmed

1.   Make the marinade: Combine the marinade ingredients, and rub on both sides of the fish; let stand for 20 minutes.

2.   Grill the fish: Place two lime slices in the cavity of each fish. Put the fish on the prepared grill and grill for 4–5 minutes. Turn with long-handled tongs and grill until done. At the same time, brush oil on scallions and grill 1–2 minutes on each side. Transfer the fish to individual plates and serve immediately with scallions.

Makes 8 servings

Serving suggestions: rice, stir-fried vegetables, vanilla ice cream topped with minced sweet Oriental ginger, including syrup, for dessert.

Fish substitutions: red snapper, rockfish

A mature white Graves, such as Latour Martillac 1983, would be an interesting matchup for this Oriental dish. *S.M.*

100

Shad Roe

Handle shad roe, available in the spring, carefully as the skin tears easily.

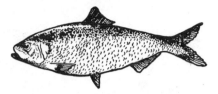

GRILLED SHAD ROE ON TOAST WITH CAPERS

4 12-ounce pieces shad roe
Melted butter or margarine for brushing roe
2 cups trimmed fresh parsley
8 slices buttered toast, trimmed
2 2-ounce cans flat anchovies, drained
1 3½-ounce jar large capers, drained

1. Brush shad roe with melted butter. Spread parsley sprigs on a prepared grill basket or the prepared grill. Place the roe on the parsley. Grill the roe for 3 minutes, turn using a long-handled spatula, and continue grilling for 3–4 minutes or until done to taste.

2. To serve, arrange hot toast on individual plates and place half of a roe piece on each slice of toast. Drizzle lightly with more melted butter. Cross 2 anchovies decoratively over the roe and sprinkle with capers.

Makes 8 servings

Serving suggestions: mixed green salad tossed with candied almonds and orange slices, grilled tomato halves.

A rosé from Provence, such as Mas de Gourgonnier 1985, stands up especially well to the roe, anchovies, and capers. *S.M.*

Shark

Shark is a firm fish and should be soaked in milk for 1 hour before cooking.

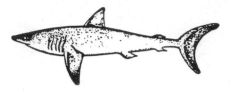

SHARK WITH BARBECUE BUTTER

BARBECUE BUTTER
½ cup (¼ pound) butter or margarine, at room temperature
1 scallion, minced
2 teaspoons prepared barbecue sauce
3 tablespoons minced cilantro

BARBECUE SAUCE
1½ cups catsup
¾ cup tomato sauce
½ cup cider vinegar
1 teaspoon soy sauce
2 cloves garlic, minced
2 teaspoons Worcestershire sauce
2 teaspoons prepared mustard
½ teaspoon salt
¼ teaspoon freshly ground pepper
2 teaspoons honey
¼ cup white wine (optional)

FISH
2 cups hickory chips
3 pounds shark steaks, cut into 8 serving pieces, about ½-¾ inch thick
Milk for soaking shark steaks
Oil for brushing fish

1. Make the barbecue butter: Soften the butter in a bowl with the back of a wooden spoon. Blend in the scallion, prepared barbecue sauce, and cilantro. Transfer to a 10-inch sheet of waxed paper. Spread the butter 1 inch thick along the edge of the paper. Roll, jelly roll style, keeping the inch thickness but shaping into a roll. Secure the ends. Refrigerate or freeze until the butter is firm. When ready to serve, unroll, discard paper, and slice butter as necessary.

2. Make the barbecue sauce: Combine all barbecue sauce ingredients in a pan and bring to a boil. Reduce the heat to a simmer and continue cooking for 5 minutes, stirring occasionally. Taste and adjust seasonings. Cool, place in a bowl, cover, and refrigerate.

3. Meanwhile, soak the hickory chips in cold water to cover for 1 hour and soak the shark steaks in milk to cover in a shallow glass dish for 1 hour.

4. Grill the fish: Drain the fish and pat dry with paper toweling. Drain the hickory chips and sprinkle over the hot coals. Replace the grill. Brush the shark steaks with oil. Grill the fish on the prepared grill for 4–8 minutes. Turn and continue grilling until the fish is just fork-tender.

5. Serve each portion of fish hot with a ½-inch slice of barbecue butter. Pass the warm barbecue sauce and extra butter slices at the table.

Makes 8 servings (2¾ cups sauce)

Serving suggestions: warm flour tortillas, grilled red and green pepper slices, grilled tomatillos or tomatoes

Fish substitutions: halibut, tuna

Barbecue sauce, with its sweet-and-sour pungency, needs a nice smooth red—try a cabernet from Spain, Jean Leon 1981, for a supple, nicely oaky partner to the hickory-flavored shark as well as the sauce. Or serve a Mexican beer such as Carta Blanca. *S.M.*

Sole

Dover sole is characterized by a delicate flavor and subtle, fine texture. It lends itself easily to accompanying many flavors.

GRILLED DOVER SOLE WITH HERBS AND MINT BUTTER

As the fish grills, some of the herbs will fall into the coals and add their own aroma as they burn.

FISH
1 recipe Basic Marinade (see Index)
3 pounds Dover sole fillets, washed and patted dry, cut into 8 serving pieces

MINT BUTTER
¾ cup (1½) sticks butter or margarine, cut into small pieces
¼ cup trimmed fresh mint sprigs
1 tablespoon crème de menthe liqueur

1 cup trimmed fresh thyme sprigs
¾ cup trimmed fresh mint sprigs
1 cup trimmed fresh parsley sprigs
Melted butter or margarine for brushing fillets

1. Marinate the fish: Pour the marinade into a large plastic bag and add the Dover sole fillets. Secure with a twister seal and turn the bag several times to make sure all fish surfaces touch the marinade. Place the bag in a bowl and let sit at room temperature for 1 hour.

2.   Meanwhile, make the mint butter: Put the butter into a blender or a food processor fitted with the steel blade. Add the mint sprigs and the crème de menthe. Process until the ingredients are well blended. Spread in a bowl, cover, and refrigerate until needed.

3.   Grill the fish: Arrange the thyme, ¾ cup mint, and parsley over the prepared grill or in a prepared grill basket. Remove the fish from the marinade, brush with butter, and place the sole fillets on the herbs. Grill without turning 2–6 minutes, or until the fillets have lost their translucence and are cooked to taste. Remove the mint butter from the refrigerator while the fillets are grilling so that the butter is soft when served. Serve the fillets hot with the mint butter.

Makes 8 servings (¾ cup mint butter)

Serving suggestions: spinach or egg linguine, grilled artichoke hearts
Fish substitutions: brill, flounder

This delicate dish calls for a classic Sancerre, a crisp sauvignon blanc–based wine from the Loire. *S.M.*

SOLE WITH CIDER AND GRILLED PEAR SLICES

MARINADE

1½ cups apple cider
1   teaspoon prepared mustard
½   teaspoon ground allspice
¼   teaspoon freshly grated nutmeg
Salt and freshly ground white pepper to taste

FISH

3   pounds sole fillets, cut into 8 serving pieces
2   cups trimmed fresh parsley
1   large onion, sliced thin
4   firm pears, cored, and sliced horizontally into rings
Melted butter or margarine for brushing pears

1.   Make the marinade: Combine the marinade ingredients and pour the marinade into a large plastic bag. Add the sole and secure the bag with a twister seal. Turn the bag several times to make sure all fish surfaces touch the marinade. Place the bag in a bowl and let sit at room temperature for 1 hour.

2.   Grill the fish: Spread the parsley over one side of a prepared grill basket and place the onion slices over the parsley. Place the sole on the bed of parsley and onion slices and close the basket. Grill the fish for 2–6 minutes, without turning, until done to taste. While the fish is cooking, brush the pear slices with melted butter and grill lightly on both sides.

3.   Serve the fish and pear slices hot with parsley and onions, discarding the very burned sprigs.

Makes 8 servings

Serving suggestions: new potatoes boiled in skins and tossed with butter and chopped chives, hot French bread

Fish substitutions: flounder, plaice, orange roughy

If you didn't bring back any French hard cider from your last trip to Normandy, try the fresh, applelike chardonnay from Alderbrook, 1985. *S.M.*

106

GRILLED SOLE FILLETS WITH HERBS

COATING

2   cups uncooked fine-grained oatmeal
4   tablespoons chopped fresh parsley
½   teaspoon dried rosemary, crumbled
    Salt and freshly ground pepper to taste
2   egg whites, lightly beaten

FISH

3   pounds sole fillets, cut into 8 serving pieces
Lemon wedges

1.   Make the coating: Combine the oatmeal, parsley, rosemary, salt, and pepper and place on a sheet of waxed paper. Put the egg whites into a shallow bowl.

2.   Brush each fillet with the egg whites and roll in the oatmeal coating, patting the oats firmly onto the fish fillets.

3.   Grill the fish: Arrange the fillets in a prepared grill basket and cook on the prepared grill for 2–6 minutes. Turn the basket and grill until the fish tests done with a fork.

4.   Place the fillets on individual plates and serve with lemon wedges.

Makes 8 servings

Serving suggestions: salad of endive and watercress, tomato soup with sage
Fish substitutions: plaice, flounder

William Hill Chardonnay, Silver Label 1986, provides just the right amount of oak to complement this unusual dish. *S.M.*

SOLE WITH PINE NUT SAUCE

This Middle Eastern sauce, like so many nut- and seed-based sauces, needs no cooking. Simply process the ingredients in the food processor or blender and heat before serving. This sauce can also be served at room temperature.

FISH
Salt and freshly ground pepper to taste
3 pounds sole fillets, cut into 8 serving pieces
½ cup fresh lemon juice

PINE NUT SAUCE
1½ cups (8 ounces) pine nuts
⅔ cup toasted bread crumbs
4 cloves garlic, peeled and quartered
5 tablespoons fresh lemon juice
2 tablespoons imported mild, good-quality olive oil
1¼ cups water (more if needed)

16 ¼-inch-thick slices lemon for grilling
Lemon wedges

1. Marinate the fish: Generously salt and pepper the fillets. Then pour the lemon juice into a plastic bag and set in a large bowl. Add the sole fillets to the bag and secure the bag with a twister seal. Turn the bag to be sure all fish surfaces touch the lemon juice. Let sit at room temperature for 15–30 minutes.

2. Meanwhile, make the sauce: Preheat the oven to 350°F to toast the pine nuts. Arrange the pine nuts in a single layer on a baking sheet and put them in oven for about 10 minutes, watching them carefully. After the first 5 minutes, check them every minute or so to make sure they don't burn. Remove from the oven as soon as they are lightly browned.

3. Reserve 1 tablespoon of the toasted pine nuts to use as garnish. Put the remaining nuts in a food processor fitted with the steel blade or in a blender along with the bread crumbs, garlic, lemon juice, olive oil, and water. Process, pulsing on and off for a minute or so, until a coarse sauce

results. If you wish to serve the sauce at room temperature, set it aside. If you plan to serve it hot, transfer it to a saucepan.

4. Grill the fish: Arrange the lemon slices in pairs on the prepared grill. Place the fillets on the lemon slices and cook for 2–6 minutes, without turning, or until they are completely cooked through and have lost their translucence. If you are serving the sauce hot, heat it in the saucepan while the fish is grilling.

5. Using two spatulas, carefully transfer the fillets to a serving platter. Spoon the room-temperature or hot pine nut sauce over the fillets and garnish with the reserved pine nuts. Pass lemon wedges at the table.

Makes 8 servings (2½ cups sauce)

Serving suggestions: tart green salad, hot French bread

Fish substitutions: orange roughy, scrod

Although thousands of complementary wines are available, I urge you to try the wonderful varietal wines of New York state and Virginia. A chardonnay, Riesling, or sauvignon blanc from those areas would be excellent with this dish. *L.S.*

Swordfish
Swordfish, a firm and mildly distinctive fish, is a favorite for grilling.

GRILLED SWORDFISH ON GRAPE LEAVES

Placing dried grapevine pieces over the hot coals adds a slightly smoky flavor to this fish.

BASTING MIXTURE
  4   tablespoons good-quality olive oil
  4   tablespoons fresh lemon juice
  1   teaspoon dried oregano, crumbled
  ¼ teaspoon salt
  ⅛ teaspoon freshly ground pepper

FISH
4–6 pieces grapevine (optional; available in Greek food stores or in backyard if you have a grapevine)
Enough large fresh pesticide- and herbicide-free grape leaves to arrange a double layer on grill basket or on grill
  3   pounds swordfish steaks, cut into 8 serving pieces about ½ inch thick
  2   lemons, sliced paper-thin
  2   lemons, cut into wedges

    1. Make the basting mixture: Whisk together the basting mixture ingredients in a shallow bowl. Brush fish generously with the mixture.

2. Grill the fish: Arrange grapevine pieces over the hot coals and replace the grill. Make a double layer of grape leaves in prepared grill basket, on both top and bottom. Place the fish in the basket with lemon slices on top and secure shut. Grill for 4–8 minutes, turn the basket, and continue grilling until done.

3. Put the swordfish pieces on individual plates and serve with lemon wedges.

Makes 8 servings

Serving suggestions: cucumber and onion salad or Greek salad, dish of olives, and crusty bread

Fish substitutions: shark, ono

This meaty fish, slightly smoky after being grilled over vine cuttings, needs a rich buttery chardonnay, such as Matanzas Creek 1985. *S.M.*

SERPENTINE SWORDFISH STRIPS

This dish is easy and fun to serve. See the accompanying illustration.

16 8-inch-long wooden barbecue skewers

MARINADE
½ cup sour cream or sour half-and-half
½ cup fresh lemon juice
½ teaspoon salt
¼ teaspoon freshly ground white pepper

FISH
3 pounds swordfish fillets, cut ¾ inch thick and as long as possible

SAUCE
2 cups sour cream or sour half-and-half
2 tablespoons fresh lemon juice
¼ teaspoon salt (more to taste)
Few grinds black pepper

1. Soak the skewers in cold water for 1 hour.
2. Make the marinade: Mix the marinade ingredients together, pour into a large plastic bag, and set the bag in a bowl.
3. Cut the swordfish steaks into strips, a scant 1 inch wide, each as long as possible. Add the strips to the marinade in the bag and secure with a twister seal. Turn the bag several times to make certain all the surfaces of the fish touch the marinade. Let sit at room temperature for 1 hour, turning occasionally.
4. While the fish marinates, make the sauce: Mix the sauce ingredients together in a small saucepan and set aside.
5. Remove the swordfish strips from the marinade and remove the skewers from the water. Thread the swordfish strips onto the skewers by weaving the strips over and under the skewers at 3-inch intervals (see illustration).

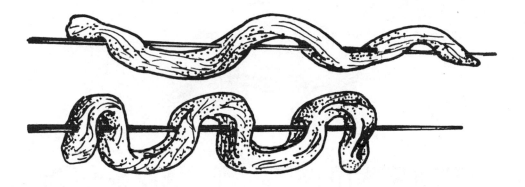

6.   Grill the fish: Place the skewered swordfish on the prepared grill and cook for about 4 minutes on each side or until the swordfish is completely cooked through and has lost its opacity.

7.   While the fish cooks, heat the sour cream sauce slowly over low heat. When the sauce is warmed, transfer it to a serving bowl and bring it to the table.

8.   When the swordfish is cooked, transfer the skewers to a serving platter and bring the platter to the table. Present the skewers topped with the sour cream sauce.

Makes 8 servings (2 cups sauce)

Serving suggestions: tart green salad, Sweet Potato and Pineapple Kabobs (see Index)

Fish substitution: shark

In spite of the sour cream and lemon juice in the marinade, a medium-priced chardonnay or sauvignon blanc would be an excellent quaffing wine. *L.S.*

Trout

Brook trout, lake trout, and rainbow trout are medium-firm fish, medium-flavored, and can be substituted for each other.

TROUT WITH SESAME SEED SAUCE

This Middle Eastern sauce is based on tahina *(sesame seed paste) and tastes like a liquid form of that Middle Eastern sweet called* halvah, *which is also tahina-based. Tahina is available at Middle Eastern grocery stores or by mail (see Appendix for sources). The sauce is made slightly piquant by the addition of a Middle Eastern hot pepper sauce called* shatta *(hot sauce), also available by mail. If shatta is unavailable, just substitute any "picante" sauce. Sesame seed sauce can be served warm, at room temperature, or even cold with cold fillets. This dish is traditionally prepared with* Mousht, *but we have substituted trout for the* Mousht, *which is unavailable in the U.S.*

FISH

1 cup imported mild, good-quality olive oil
6 tablespoons fresh lemon juice
8 10- to 12-ounce rainbow trout, scaled and gutted, heads and tails intact

SESAME SEED SAUCE

2 tablespoons vegetable oil
6 cloves garlic, minced
¼ cup chopped fresh parsley
1 teaspoon salt
¼ teaspoon ground coriander
1 cup tahina
1 cup cold water

¼ cup fresh lemon juice
1½ teaspoons shatta (available in Middle Eastern markets and by mail; see Appendix) or other hot pepper sauce

Salt and freshly ground pepper to taste

GARNISHES
3 tablespoons sesame seeds
3–4 tablespoons shatta (available in Middle Eastern markets and by mail; see Appendix) or other hot pepper sauce
3 tablespoons finely chopped fresh parsley
Lemon wedges

1. Marinate the fish: Pour the olive oil and lemon juice into a large plastic bag and set the bag in a bowl. Place the fish in the bag, secure with a twister seal, and turn the bag several times to make sure all fish surfaces touch the marinade. Let sit at room temperature for 1 hour.

2. Meanwhile, make the sauce: Heat oil in a small saucepan over medium heat. Add the garlic, parsley, salt, and coriander and sauté for about 5 minutes, watching carefully so the mixture does not burn. Allow to cool slightly.

3. Scrape the garlic mixture into a food processor fitted with the steel blade or into a blender. Add the tahina along with the cold water, lemon juice, and shatta. Process until a smooth paste results.

4. Grill the fish: Remove the fish from the marinade and liberally salt and pepper the insides of the fish. Place the fish in a prepared grill basket and cook for 4–8 minutes until one side has browned. Then turn the basket and grill until the second side has browned. Transfer the fish carefully to a serving platter.

5. Meanwhile, toast the sesame seeds: Place the seeds in a single layer in a small saucepan and set over medium heat. Watch carefully and have a wooden spoon handy. They should start to brown in a minute or two. As soon as they begin to brown, stir them with the wooden spoon, cook another minute, until they're golden, then remove from heat. Transfer to a small bowl and set on the table along with the shatta, chopped parsley, and lemon wedges.

6. Transfer the sesame seed sauce to a saucepan and heat, stirring often and watching carefully so it does not burn. Then spoon the warmed sauce into a serving bowl and place on the table. If desired, this sauce may be served at room temperature.

7. To serve, transfer each fish carefully to a dinner plate. Spoon a mound of sesame seed sauce to one side of the fish on each plate. Instruct your guests to top the sesame seed sauce with a large spoonful of shatta, a sprinkle of sesame seeds, and some chopped parsley. Pass the lemon wedges.

Makes 8 servings (2¼ cups sauce)

Serving suggestions: cracked wheat salad (tabbouleh), salad of peeled, seeded, and chopped cucumber, plain yogurt, a little finely chopped garlic, and salt.

Fish substitution: 8 12- to 16-ounce scaled and gutted black sea bass

This complex sauce for trout calls for something simple—beer! Or, if you're adventurous, choose one of the Israeli white wines. They have a lot of inherent sweetness due to so much sun. *L.S.*

GRILLED TROUT WITH TWO CHEESES

MARINADE

½ cup good-quality olive oil
4 tablespoons fresh lemon juice
1½ cups Portuguese or other white wine
3 cloves garlic, minced
4 tablespoons minced fresh parsley

FISH

8 8- to 10-ounce trout, cleaned and scaled, heads and tails left on
1 onion, sliced thin
Salt and freshly ground pepper to taste
¼ pound Parmesan cheese, grated
¼ pound Romano cheese, grated

1. Make the marinade: Combine the olive oil, lemon juice, wine, garlic, and parsley and divide between two large plastic bags; place the bags in a large bowl. Place 4 trout in each bag and divide the onion slices between the bags. Secure the bags with twister seals. Turn the bags a few times to make sure all fish surfaces touch the marinade. Let sit at room temperature for 1 hour.

2. Remove the fish from the marinade and salt and pepper each liberally inside and outside.

3. Grill the fish: Arrange the fish on greased foil placed on the prepared grill. Sprinkle with cheese, adhering cheese to the fish. Cook for about 4–8 minutes, until done.

4. Serve the fish on hot plates immediately.

Makes 8 servings

Serving suggestions: garlic mashed potatoes, mixed endive salad, sliced beets, green olives

Fish substitutions: walleye pike, rainbow trout

A light and refreshing 1986 soave from Anselmi has just the right amount of flavor to balance with this simple dish. *S.M.*

ST. PETER'S FISH ON THE GRILL

This dish is based on a fish with the scientific name Telapia galilaea, *which is abundantly available in the Sea of Galilee. Although the fish is served primarily by Hebrews—it's known in Israel as* Mushat b'Shalem—*and by Moslems—it's known in Arab countries as* Mousht—*Christians have nicknamed it St. Peter's fish for biblical reasons.*

According to John 21:6, St. Peter and his friends went fishing one day but came home empty-handed. Learning that the fishing trip had been fruitless, Jesus intervened, instructing the fishermen to "cast the net on the right side of the boat, and you will find some."

According to the story, the net was cast and immediately grew so heavy with 153 Telapia galilaea *inside that it could not be hauled in. Jesus then told St. Peter to try hauling the net in, and following Jesus's instruction, St. Peter was able to bring the whole net ashore by himself.*

Telapia galilaea *is also thought to be the fish that Jesus advised St. Peter to pull out of the water in Matthew 17:27—the one that contained the shekel needed by St. Peter for taxes.*

Telapia galilaea, *a very flat fish, also figures in Jewish legend: it is said to have flattened when its ancestors were split in two lengthwise, during the parting of the Red Sea.*

Whatever you believe, you'll probably want to prepare the fish as it is served all over the Middle East. The most common preparation, made on the shores of the Sea of Galilee, involves stuffing the fish with onions and parsley, brushing it with oil and fresh lemon juice, adding salt and pepper, and grilling it over glowing coals.

Since you will have difficulty getting this breamlike fish in the U.S., we suggest substituting rainbow trout.

1   cup imported mild, good-quality olive oil
6   tablespoons fresh lemon juice
8   10- to 12-ounce gutted and scaled rainbow trout, heads and tails left on
2   pounds medium-sized onions, cut into ¼-inch-thick slices
Salt and freshly ground pepper to taste
2   cups finely chopped fresh parsley
Lemon wedges

1.   Marinate the fish: Mix the olive oil and lemon juice in a large plastic bag and set the bag in a large bowl. Place the trout and onion slices in the bag and secure with a twister seal. Turn the bag a few times to make sure that all fish and onion surfaces touch the marinade. Let sit at room temperature for 1 hour.

2.   Grill the onions: Remove the onion slices from the marinade and salt and pepper them lightly. Place the onions on the prepared grill and cook for about 6 minutes, watching carefully and turning the onions with a spatula as soon as one side has browned. Remove them from the grill.

3.   Remove the fish from the marinade and salt and pepper each liberally inside. Sprinkle 2 tablespoons of the chopped parsley on the inside of each fish, then arrange the onion slices on the parsley. Sprinkle 2 tablespoons of the parsley over the onion slices in each fish. Skewer each fish to close it.

4.   Place the fish in an oiled grill basket and set on the prepared grill. Cook the fish for 4–8 minutes or until it is browned on one side. Transfer the fish to a serving platter and serve immediately. Pass a platter of lemon wedges.

Makes 8 servings

Serving suggestions: Potato Salad with Gorgonzola Cheese and Pine Nuts (see Index) or homemade baked beans, and coleslaw

Fish substitution: 8 12- to 16-ounce dressed, black sea bass

The simplicity of this dish calls for a chardonnay or an intense sauvignon blanc. For the adventuresome diner, I suggest an Italian Pinot Grigio or Pomino. *L.S.*

LAKE TROUT ON ROSE LEAVES
SERVED WITH ROSE BUTTER

Rose petals and leaves grown for the express purpose of being used as food should be free of herbicides and pesticides.

ROSE BUTTER

½ teaspoon rose water (available from Maid of Scandinavia; see Appendix)

½ cup (¼ pound) butter or margarine, at room temperature, cut into ½-inch chunks

2 tablespoons minced fresh parsley

FISH

Enough well-washed rose leaves on completely clean short stems to arrange in a double layer in a grill basket

8 8- to 10-ounce lake trout, cleaned, head discarded

2 large oranges, cut into 16 thin slices

Melted butter or margarine for brushing fish

1 teaspoon dried tarragon, crumbled

½ cup pesticide- and herbicide-free rose petals, completely clean, for garnish (optional)

1. Make the rose butter: Blend rose water and butter in a food processor fitted with the steel blade. Add parsley and combine. Mound the butter in a small bowl, cover, and refrigerate. Remove from refrigerator 45 minutes before serving time so that the butter will be at room temperature.

2. Grill the fish: Arrange a double layer of rose leaves on one side of an oiled grill basket or on the prepared grill. Place 2 orange slices inside each fish. Brush the fish with melted butter and arrange the fish on the rose leaves. Sprinkle the fish with the tarragon. Grill for 4–8 minutes, depending on the thickness of the fish. Turn over and continue grilling until done to taste or test with a fork to see if fish is just beginning to flake.

3. Put the fish on individual plates and top each with a dollop of rose butter. Sprinkle with rose petals if desired.

Makes 8 servings

Serving suggestions: wild and white rice, cruditées, hearts of palm salad

Fish substitution: brook trout

The floral scents present in the rose butter are perfectly complemented by similar essences in German Rieslings. A 1983 Kabinett, the driest, from the Wehlener Sonnenuhr vineyard of J. J. Prum, would make an interesting combination. *S.M.*

TROUT IN A BACON BLANKET

This is a Mormon specialty from Utah. It is usually served with a lemon butter sauce, but we think just serving lemon wedges is sufficient. If you wish to serve the sauce, simply mix ½ cup melted butter or margarine with 2–3 tablespoons lemon juice and ⅛ teaspoon each salt and freshly ground pepper.

1   cup imported mild, good-quality olive oil
6   tablespoons fresh lemon juice
8   12-ounce trout, scaled and gutted, heads and tails left on
Salt and freshly ground pepper to taste
16   slices bacon, cooked until crisp
40   slices bacon, half-cooked but still limp
40   round wooden toothpicks
Lemon wedges

1. Marinate the fish: Combine the oil and lemon juice in a large plastic bag and place the bag in a large bowl. Place the fish in the bag, secure the bag with a twister seal, and turn the bag a few times to make sure the marinade touches the fish inside and out. Let sit at room temperature for 1 hour.

2. Remove the fish from the marinade and lightly pat the outsides of the fish with paper towels. Salt and pepper the insides of the fish heavily, then put 2 slices of crisply cooked bacon inside each fish.

3. Grill the fish: Wrap each fish completely in half-cooked bacon, using 5 slices per fish. Fasten the bacon strips with round wooden toothpicks. Arrange the fish in a grill basket.

4. Place the grill basket on the prepared grill and cook for about 5 minutes on each side or until brown. The bacon should be crisp.

5. Transfer the fish to a serving platter and serve. Pass a plate of lemon wedges.

Makes 8 servings

Serving suggestions: Potato Salad with Gorgonzola Cheese and Pine Nuts (see Index) or homemade baked beans, and coleslaw

Fish substitution: 8 12- to 16-ounce dressed black sea bass

Unless you're Mormon and don't drink alcohol, don't deprive yourself of a chardonnay, Riesling (dry), or sauvignon blanc. Or you can just slip a few cans of beer or a bottle of bubbly into the old trout stream. *L.S.*

Tuna

Tuna is a delicious, firm fish and a favorite for grilling.

GRILLED TUNA SANDWICHES

3   cups mesquite chips

ROLLS
½   cup (¼ pound) butter or margarine
½   teaspoon minced garlic
8   seeded kaiser rolls, split

FISH
8   ¼- to ½-inch-thick slices tuna
Melted butter or margarine for brushing tuna
1   large red onion, sliced thin
8   crisp, trimmed lettuce leaves
2   large tomatoes, sliced
Mayonnaise or coarsely ground mustard (optional)

    1.   Soak the mesquite chips in cold water to cover for 1 hour.
    2.   Prepare the rolls: Melt the butter in small saucepan over low heat, mixing in the garlic as the butter melts. Remove from the heat. Brush the cut sides of the rolls with the garlic butter. Grill the rolls slightly, cut side down, on the prepared grill. Put the rolls on a tray and cover with aluminum foil.
    3.   Grill the fish: Brush the tuna slices with melted butter. Drain the mesquite chips and sprinkle them over the ashen coals. Grill the onions briefly on both sides or place under the tuna and grill together. Grill the tuna for 4–5 minutes, brush with butter, turn, and continue grilling on the other side until done to taste. Transfer the tuna slices to a platter and assemble the sandwiches immediately.

4.   Place a lettuce leaf on the bottom half of each roll, then arrange an onion slice and a tuna slice over the lettuce. Top with a tomato slice and brush with mayonnaise or mustard if desired.

Makes 8 servings

Serving suggestions: dill pickles, potato chips, grilled potato skins with sour cream, creamy coleslaw

Fish substitutions: swordfish, marlin

These grilled tuna sandwiches call for a simple, fruity chardonnay, such as Mountain View 1986. *S.M.*

GRILLED TUNA WITH RED PEPPER SAUCE

RED PEPPER SAUCE

3 large red bell peppers
3 tablespoons fresh lemon juice
1 cup (½ pound) butter or margarine, cut into 1-inch pieces
¾ teaspoon dried tarragon, crumbled
½ teaspoon dried thyme, crumbled
¼ teaspoon salt
⅛ teaspoon freshly ground white pepper

FISH

½ cup dried thyme for sprinkling on hot coals
3 pounds tuna, cut into 8 steaks
Good-quality olive oil for brushing tuna

1. Make the sauce: Grill the peppers on the prepared grill, turning frequently using long-handled tongs. This will take about 8–10 minutes; all sides should be charred and blistered. Immediately place the peppers in a large plastic bag, and secure shut with a twister seal. Let stand for 10–12 minutes.

2. Remove the peppers from the bag, cut off the tops, and remove the skins by rubbing gently under cold water. Discard the seeds. Slice the peppers and puree in a food processor fitted with the steel blade or in a blender.

3. Blend together the lemon juice and pepper puree in a saucepan. Cook over medium heat for 5 minutes and remove from the heat. Using a wire whisk, incorporate the butter. Whisk in the tarragon, thyme, salt, and pepper. The sauce should be served immediately, so grill the fish while completing the sauce.

4. Grill the fish: Sprinkle the dried thyme over the hot coals and replace the grill. Brush the tuna with oil on both sides and cook on the prepared grill over ashen coals for about 4 minutes on each side, depending

on the thickness of the tuna. Do not cook the tuna all the way through; it should be served medium-rare or to taste. To serve, place the tuna on a plate and spoon the sauce down the center.

Makes 8 servings (2½ cups sauce)

Serving suggestions: lettuce with avocado and mango, warm muffins, grilled red onion slices

Fish substitutions: marlin, shark

Richly oaky, yet with good acidity, the Kendall-Jackson Proprietor's Reserve Chardonnay 1985 is a big, buttery wine, a textbook match with the meaty tuna and rich red pepper puree. *S.M.*

Turbot
Turbot is a lean fish with a rich, delicate flavor.

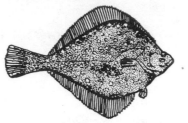

TURBOT FILLETS WITH TURKISH HAZELNUT SAUCE

This hazelnut sauce is a Turkish version of the nut-based sauces served all over the Middle East. Like all of those sauces, it is made quickly and needs only to be heated, not cooked.

TURKISH HAZELNUT SAUCE
1½ cups plus 1 teaspoon blanched hazelnuts
1 cup fresh bread crumbs
8 cloves garlic
½ cup white vinegar
½ cup mild, good-quality olive oil
2 large handfuls parsley, stems removed
1 teaspoon salt
1¼ cups water

FISH
16 ¼-inch-thick slices lemon for grilling
3 pounds turbot fillets, cut into 8 serving pieces

1. Make the sauce: Toast the hazelnuts: Preheat the oven to 350°F. Place the hazelnuts in a single layer on a baking sheet and place in the oven for 5 minutes. Check to see if they've begun to brown. If not, toast them a few minutes longer, checking often. As soon as they begin to brown lightly, remove them from the oven. They will continue browning slightly once they're away from the heat. Then measure out 3 tablespoons, chop coarsely, and reserve for garnish.

2. Place the remaining 1⅓ cups toasted hazelnuts, bread crumbs, garlic, vinegar, olive oil, parsley, salt, and 1 cup of the water in a blender or a food processor fitted with the steel blade. Process until a coarse puree results. The puree should be thick but liquid enough to pour. If it is not, add the remaining ¼ cup water and process again.

3. Grill the fish: Place the lemon slices in pairs on the prepared grill and arrange the turbot fillets over the lemon slices. Grill the fillets 3–6 minutes, without turning, or until the fillets have lost their translucence and are cooked through.

4. Meanwhile, transfer the sauce to a small, heavy-bottomed saucepan and heat, stirring occasionally. Check sauce consistency. If too thick, add a little water. When hot, spoon the sauce into a serving bowl and garnish with the reserved chopped hazelnuts.

5. Using two spatulas, carefully transfer the turbot fillets to a serving platter, discarding the lemon slices. Serve the fillets topped with a few spoonfuls of sauce.

Makes 8 servings (3 cups sauce)

Serving suggestions: Sweet Potato and Pineapple Kabobs (see Index), tart green salad

Fish substitutions: orange roughy, ono, scrod, ocean perch

The combination of this simple sauce and the turbot would be enhanced by a wine that has a slightly nutty taste. I suggest serving a sauvignon blanc with some semillon in it. French wines are not necessary. Choose Australian examples if desired. California wines such as Creston Manor and San Luis Obispo would be ideal. *L.S.*

TURBOT WITH CUMIN

This dish is based on a Moroccan preparation in which a whole fish is spread, inside and out, with a cumin/garlic paste topping. Our version for the grill uses a meaty fillet that is spread with the paste. Since the fillet is not turned, the paste stays intact on top and is attractive when served. This easy, delicious dish is as good cold as it is hot.

1	tablespoon plus ¾ teaspoon ground cumin
1	tablespoon plus 1½ teaspoons paprika
9	cloves garlic, peeled and quartered
¼	teaspoon salt
¼	teaspoon freshly ground pepper
3	large handfuls parsley, stems removed
6	tablespoons imported mild, good-quality olive oil
16	¼-inch-thick slices lemon for grilling fish
3	pounds turbot fillets, cut into 8 serving pieces

1. Combine the cumin, paprika, garlic, salt, pepper, parsley, and oil in a food processor fitted with the steel blade. Process until an oily puree results.

2. Spread the top of each fillet lightly with the cumin/garlic paste. Arrange the lemon slices in pairs on the prepared grill. Arrange the fillets on the lemon slices and grill without turning for about 6 minutes or until the fish has lost its translucence and is just cooked through. Using two spatulas, carefully transfer the fillets to a serving platter. Discard the lemon slices. Serve immediately.

Makes 8 servings

Serving suggestions: noodles tossed with a small amount of butter or margarine, green salad

Fish substitutions: scrod, ono, orange roughy

A Vina Esmeralda by Torres would be ideal with this dish. Or, if you wish to serve beer, an ale or a pilsner-style beer would be satisfactory. *L.S.*

Whitefish

Both whitefish fillets and whole fish work well on the grill.

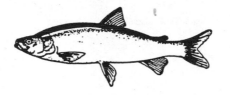

WHITEFISH FILLETS WITH PISTACHIO, GARNISHED WITH SKEWERED FRUIT

This elegant dish is Moroccan in origin, but we have changed it considerably, while retaining the original flavors, in adapting it for the grill. The original recipe calls for a large shad to be stuffed with dates, figs, prunes, and apricots, each of which has been previously stuffed with a pistachio nut mixture. Since large fish do not fit into standard-sized fish baskets and can't be turned on the grill, we use whitefish fillets that are spread with the pistachio mixture, then grilled without turning. The dried fruits also are stuffed with the mixture, then brushed with honey and placed on the grill for just a moment or until they are warm. Each guest is served one pistachio-topped fillet and one skewer of stuffed dried fruits.

8   8-inch-long wooden barbecue skewers

MARINADE
¾   cup imported, mild, good-quality olive oil
¼   cup fresh lemon juice
¾   teaspoon salt

FISH
3   pounds whitefish fillets, cut into 8 serving pieces

PISTACHIO PASTE

¾ cup cooked rice
6 ounces pistachio nuts, chopped fine (1½ cups)
6 tablespoons butter or margarine
1½ teaspoons sugar
⅜ teaspoon ground cinnamon
⅜ teaspoon ground allspice
⅛ teaspoon ground ginger
Few drops water to make paste spreadable (if needed)

FRUIT

8 large pitted dates
8 large dried apricots
8 large pitted prunes
8 large figs with hard stems snipped off
Honey for brushing skewered fruit

16 ¼-inch-thick slices lemon for grilling fillets

1. Soak the skewers in cold water to cover for 1 hour before using.

2. Make the marinade: Mix the olive oil, lemon juice, and salt in a large plastic bag. Set the bag in a bowl and add the whitefish fillets. Secure the bag with a twister seal and turn the bag several times to make sure all fish surfaces touch the marinade. Let sit at room temperature for 1 hour, turning the bag occasionally.

3. Meanwhile, make the pistachio paste: Combine the rice, pistachios, butter, sugar, cinnamon, allspice, ginger, and if needed, a few drops of water. Mix well to make a spreadable paste. Place the dates, apricots, prunes, and figs in a saucepan, cover with water, and heat to a boil. Immediately drain the fruit and allow to cool. When cool, stuff the fruit with the pistachio mixture, using ½–1 teaspoon stuffing per piece. Remove the skewers from the water and thread four pieces of fruit (one date, one apricot, one fig, and one prune) on each skewer. Brush with honey on all sides and reserve.

4. Grill the fish: Remove the fillets from the marinade and lay them flat on a large tray. Blot the tops of each fillet slightly with paper towels,

then press 2–3 tablespoons of pistachio paste onto the top of each fillet, covering it as completely as possible. Arrange the lemon slices in pairs on the prepared grill. Place one fillet on each pair of lemon slices. Grill for 4–8 minutes without turning.

    5.   About 2 minutes before the fillets have finished cooking, place the skewered fruit on the grill and grill for a minute on each side.

    6.   Using two spatulas, carefully transfer the fillets to a serving platter. Arrange the fruit skewers attractively on the platter. Serve each guest a pistachio-topped fillet and a skewer of stuffed dried fruit.

Makes 8 servings

Serving suggestions: chilled marinated fresh asparagus spears, hot French bread

Fish substitution: scrod

The Moroccans, who drink fermented mare or camel's milk, are not known as wine producers. And since mare and camel's milk are not available in American supermarkets, I suggest drinking beer, such as those 25-ounce cans from Foster's of Australia. The really adventurous might want to try a Manzanilla, which is considered the driest of sherries, although it is produced outside the Jerez de la Frontera in Sanlúcar de Barremeda. Since Morocco is only a 45-minute hydrofoil trip from Spain, and since Spanish wines are so popular in Morocco, additional choices might be Spanish wines from producers such as Torres, Marques de Riscal Rueda, or Pedro Domeq. L.S.

WHITEFISH FILLETS WITH BLACK CAVIAR BUTTER

The elegant butter served with this dish is made from whipping cream in a food processor or blender. The delicate, newborn butter is then mixed with black lumpfish caviar—the kind that's available in supermarkets and relatively inexpensive—and served at room temperature, melting over the hot fillets. Although the dish can be made successfully with commercial butter, the homemade variety is extra-delicate and makes for interesting dinner conversation ("What? You made your own butter?") as well.

FISH
1 recipe Basic Marinade (see Index)
3 pounds whitefish fillets, cut into 8 serving pieces

HOMEMADE BUTTER
2 cups whipping cream, at least 1 day old
1½ cups ice water, containing some small ice chunks
1 2-ounce jar black lumpfish caviar

16 ¼-inch-thick slices lemon for grilling fish
Lemon wedges

    1. Marinate the fish: Pour the marinade into a large plastic bag and add the whitefish. Secure with a twister seal and turn the bag several times to make sure all fish surfaces touch the marinade. Place the bag in a bowl and let sit at room temperature for 1 hour.

    2. Meanwhile, make the homemade butter: Place the whipping cream in a food processor and turn on for a few seconds or until the cream is stiffly whipped. Turn on the motor again and pour in ¾ cup of the ice water. Let the motor run for 3 minutes. Add the remaining ¾ cup ice water and let the motor run for another minute or 2 and listen for the sound of the motor groaning slightly. When you hear it, turn the processor off and look at the cream. If it has a curdled, spoiled appearance, the butter has "come," as our great-grandmothers used to say to describe the cream-into-butter process. It will not look like butter at all, but have faith; this is the first step. It may take

even longer than the 5 or 6 minutes it usually takes. If so, relax. Just let the motor continue to run and check the container contents occasionally. The cream will turn to butter eventually. (Beats churning by hand, doesn't it?) As soon as the cream has a curdled, spoiled appearance, transfer it to a strainer and gently press out all the water, using either your fingers or the back of a wooden spoon. After a minute or so of gentle pressure, the mixture will begin to look and feel like butter.

3. Transfer the butter to a small serving bowl and reserve for a minute at room temperature. You will have a scant cup of butter. Dump the contents of the lumpfish caviar jar into a strainer and hold it under gently running tap water for a minute or two or until the black dye washes off and the water runs clear. Mix 2 tablespoons of the caviar into the soft butter. Taste and add more caviar if desired.

4. Grill the fish: Arrange the lemon slices in pairs on the prepared grill. Place one whitefish fillet on each pair of lemon slices. Grill for 8 minutes, without turning, or until the fillets have lost their translucence and are slightly browned on the edges.

5. When the fillets are cooked, transfer them to a serving platter and garnish platter with lemon wedges. Spoon 1–2 tablespoons of the caviar butter onto each hot fillet and serve with lemon wedges.

Makes 8 servings (1 cup butter)

Serving suggestions: baked potatoes, split and topped with a small amount of the caviar butter if desired.

Fish substitutions: rainbow trout, lake trout, sunfish

Any white wine, ranging from champagne to a medium-sweet Riesling, would go well with this entree. If you would like to be a little daring, serve a rosé made from the cabernet, the Pinot Noir, or the zinfandel grape. Whatever your choice, serve the wine slightly chilled. *L.S.*

WHITEFISH WITH LICHEES AND SHIITAKE MUSHROOMS

MARINADE

2 cloves garlic, minced
1½ cups dry white wine
¼ cup soy sauce
1 teaspoon brown sugar
4 scallions, minced
1 teaspoon Oriental sesame oil

FISH

3 pounds whitefish fillets with skin, cut into 8 serving pieces
3 oranges, sliced thin (you'll need 16 slices altogether)
¾ pound fresh shiitake mushrooms or white button mushrooms, trimmed
Oil for brushing mushrooms
1 16-ounce can lichee nuts, drained
Orange slices for garnish

1. Make the marinade: Combine the marinade ingredients. Pour the marinade into a large plastic bag and add the whitefish. Secure with a twister seal and turn the bag several times to make sure all fish surfaces touch the marinade. Place the bag in a bowl and let sit at room temperature for 1 hour.

2. Grill the fish: Arrange the orange slices in pairs on the prepared grill. Place one whitefish fillet on each pair of orange slices. Grill for 4–8 minutes, without turning, or until the fish has lost its translucence and is slightly browned on the edges.

3. Grill the mushrooms: Brush the mushrooms caps with oil and grill for about 1 minute or until done to taste.

4. Transfer the whitefish to a serving platter. Sprinkle with the drained lichees and grilled mushrooms and garnish with extra orange slices.

Makes 8 servings

Serving suggestions: wonton soup, grilled leeks, stir-fried green bell pepper strips

Fish substitution: brook trout

With this dish, try an Alsatian Pinot Blanc—Hugel Cuvee les Amours 1985 would be great. *S.M.*

WHITEFISH WITH CHICAGO SAUCE

The word Chicago *is really a corruption of an Indian word* Che Ca Gou, *which meant "great" or "powerful" and which the Illinois Indians used alternately to refer to a large fort or to the wild onions that grew along the banks of what became the Chicago River. Since wild onions are in shorter supply today than they once were, we suggest you substitute small, tender leeks for the once plentiful young, green, odoriferous shoots.*

CHICAGO SAUCE

1	tablespoon olive oil
3	tablespoons butter or margarine
1	large shallot *or* 2 small shallots, minced
¾	cup chopped wild onion or small leek, both white and green parts
1	tablespoon flour
½	teaspoon dried tarragon, crumbled
¼	teaspoon salt
1	cup whipping cream

FISH

3	pounds whitefish fillets, cut into 8 serving pieces
	Melted butter or margarine for brushing fillets
16	¼-inch-thick slices orange for grilling fish
8	wild onions, trimmed, for garnish

1. Make the sauce: Heat the oil and butter in a skillet. Add shallots and wild onions and simmer for 2 minutes or until tender. Whisk in the flour and cook until it is absorbed. Season with tarragon and salt. Stir in the cream and reduce the heat. Simmer until slightly thickened and warm.

2. Grill the fish: Brush the fish with melted butter. Arrange the orange slices in pairs on the prepared grill. Place a whitefish fillet on each pair of orange slices and grill for 4–8 minutes, without turning, or until the fillets have lost their translucence and are slightly browned on the edges.

3. When the fillets are cooked, transfer them to a serving platter and spoon the warm sauce over the fish. Arrange the wild onions across the fish as a garnish.

Makes 8 servings (1½ cups sauce)

Serving suggestions: tossed spinach/orange salad, grilled sweet potatoes

Fish substitutions: haddock, trout

A Loire Valley white, Pouilly Fumé Michel Redde 1986, provides a subtly herbaceous counterpoint to the wild onions. *S.M.*

WHITEFISH FILLETS WITH DARK RAISIN SAUCE

DARK RAISIN SAUCE

2 tablespoons butter or margarine
4 teaspoons flour
1 cup beef broth (canned broth can be used, but do not use beef bouillon)
1¼ cups dry white wine
1½ ounces commercial gingersnaps (6 2-inch cookies), crumbled
½ cup dark raisins
¼ cup sugar
1 tablespoon fresh lemon juice
¼ teaspoon salt
¾ cup water

FISH

3 pounds whitefish fillets, cut into 8 serving pieces
16 ¼-inch-thick slices orange, for grilling fish

1. Make the sauce: Melt the butter in a large saucepan over medium heat. Add the flour and stir with a wooden spoon until the mixture turns golden brown. Stir in the beef broth and white wine and simmer over low heat, stirring often, until the mixture thickens slightly. Add the gingersnaps, raisins, sugar, lemon juice, and salt. Return to a simmer and cook for about 5 minutes, stirring often to make sure the mixture does not burn. Add ½ cup of the water and stir. Remove from heat.

2. Grill the fish: Place the orange slices in pairs on the prepared grill. Carefully arrange the whitefish fillets on the orange slices, skin side down. Cook for about 4–8 minutes, without turning, or until the fish is cooked through and no longer opaque.

3. While the fillets are cooking, reheat the sauce to a simmer and check the consistency. If necessary, add the remaining ¼ cup water and return to a simmer. Transfer to a serving bowl.

4.   Carefully remove the fillets from the grill, discarding the orange slices, and place on a serving platter. Serve immediately, topping each fillet with a liberal spoonful of raisin sauce. Pass additional raisin sauce.

Makes 8 servings (3 cups sauce)

Serving suggestions: boiled new potatoes, steamed broccoli

Fish substitutions: scrod, catfish

The gingersnaps, raisins, and lemon juice require a fruity and soft wine like a chenin blanc, a Johannisberg Riesling, a Muscat de Frontignan from Australia, a white zinfandel, or a blush wine. *L.S.*

FISH SALAD IN A TOASTED LOAF

This company dish, made of leftovers, consists of a round white or sourdough loaf that is hollowed out and filled with a delicious fish salad. The filled loaf is served cut into wedges. Hollowed-out breads filled with different preparations such as this one were popular in the 1950s and are now coming back into style. Note that, unlike most of the recipes in this book, this dish will serve only six.

DRESSING
1   egg
2   tablespoons red wine vinegar
1   cup vegetable oil
¼   medium-sized onion
2   scallions, cut into 1-inch lengths
Large handful fresh parsley
2   tablespoons sweet pickle relish
¼   cup pimiento-stuffed green olives
1   tablespoon fresh lemon juice
1   teaspoon sugar
½   teaspoon salt (or to taste)

FISH
2   cups flaked leftover grilled fish
½   cup coarsely chopped pecans

TOASTED LOAF
1   1¼- to 1½-pound round bread (use white or sourdough if possible; otherwise substitute rye or pumpernickel)
3   tablespoons melted butter or margarine

    1.   Make the dressing: Place egg, wine vinegar, and ¼ cup of the oil in a food processor fitted with the steel blade and process for a few seconds to combine. Measure out the remaining ¾ cup oil and turn on the motor; add the oil in a thin, steady stream with the motor running. When all the oil has been added, turn off the motor. (You can use a blender for this step.)

2.   Add onion, scallion lengths, and parsley to the food processor and process until these ingredients are chopped coarse. Then add relish, green olives, lemon juice, sugar, and salt and pulse a few times to chop the olives coarse and combine seasonings.

3.   Make the salad: Place flaked fish and pecans in a serving bowl. Stir in ½ cup of the dressing and toss lightly to combine. Taste, then add a few more tablespoons of dressing if desired. Reserve the remaining dressing for another use, such as tuna, salmon, or chicken salad. Let sit at room temperature until ready to stuff the bread.

4.   Hollow out the bread: Preheat the oven to 350°F. With a small, serrated knife, cut a 4-inch circle in the top of the bread (use a 4-inch cardboard circle as a guide for the knife if desired). Carefully cut the bread under the circle so the circle can be lifted off the top of the bread.

5.   Using your fingers, carefully pull out the center of the bread, hollowing out the shell. Leave no more than a ½-inch-thick bread crust.

6.   Using a pastry brush, brush the inside of the hollowed-out bread and the inside of the 4-inch circle with melted butter. Place the bread in the oven for 10 to 15 minutes or until the outside crust is crisp.

7.   Immediately remove the bread and 4-inch circle from the oven and spoon the fish salad into the bread. Top with the 4-inch circle and serve immediately, cut into wedges.

Makes 6 servings (1¼ cups dressing, 3 cups fish salad)

Serving suggestions: cold vegetables tossed with vinaigrette or green salad

Fish substitutions: use any leftover fish or shellfish such as chopped shrimp, lobster, crab, or squid steaks

I specifically recommend a Spanish white wine called Marques de Riscal Rueda. It's a dry white wine with a medium body and a strong almond flavor—strong enough to stand up to this mélange of tastes. Other suggestions include a California sauvignon blanc or a Muscadet from the Loire in France. Both of these are also assertive enough to stand up to the strong ingredients in this dish. *L.S.*

REGRILLED FISH PATTIES

These delicious patties make use of leftover grilled fish. When grilling these patties, remember that the fish is already cooked and must be watched carefully so it does not burn. Note that, unlike most recipes in this book, this serves only four.

2 cups flaked leftover grilled fish
1½ cups fine fresh bread crumbs
2 tablespoons evaporated milk or cream
4 eggs
4 scallions, chopped fine
¼ cup dried currants
6 tablespoons coarsely chopped pecans
1 teaspoon ground allspice
½ teaspoon salt
Few grinds of pepper
Oil for brushing patties

1. Combine all ingredients except the oil in a large bowl.
2. Scoop out a scant ½ cup and form into a compact, 3-inch-diameter round patty. Repeat with the remaining mixture; you should have eight patties.
3. Brush the patties with oil and place on the prepared grill. Grill for about 3 minutes on one side, then brush with oil and carefully turn the patties using a spatula. Cook for an additional 3 minutes or until done. Transfer to a serving platter and serve immediately.

4 servings (2 patties per person)

Serving suggestions: french-fried or baked potatoes

Fish substitutions: any leftover cooked fish or shellfish such as shrimp, lobster, crab, or squid steaks

Break out the beer when the grilling is done. *L.S.*

GRILLED FISH SANDWICHES
IN A TOAST BASKET

If you ever find yourself with a large amount of leftover grilled fish on hand, use this attractive presentation to serve fish sandwiches.

Sliced bread of your choice
Mayonnaise (preferably homemade)
Sliced cold grilled fish
Finely chopped fresh parsley or chives
Toast basket from Grilled Apple Slices in a Cinnamon Toast Basket (see Index), omitting butter and cinnamon sugar

1.   Trim the crusts from the bread and spread a thin layer of mayonnaise on one side of each slice. Place fish slices between 2 slices.
2.   Spread a thin layer of mayonnaise around the rim of each sandwich and dip each side in the parsley or chives.
3.   Fill the toast basket with the sandwiches, rims up, and serve.

Serving suggestion: Raw vegetable platter: pickles, celery, carrots, cucumbers, green pepper

SHRIMP FAJITAS

FAJITA SAUCE
  3   tablespoons bacon drippings
  1   red onion, sliced thin
  3   cloves garlic, minced
  4   tablespoons dark brown sugar
2½ tablespoons cider vinegar
 ½ cup catsup
  1   cup beer
 ⅛ teaspoon salt
  1   teaspoon Worcestershire sauce

SHELLFISH
  4   limes, sliced thin
1½ pounds large shrimp, peeled and deveined
 ½ teaspoon red pepper flakes
 ½ teaspoon paprika
  4   large onions, sliced thin
Good-quality olive oil for brushing onions
  8   flour tortillas
Salt and freshly ground pepper to taste

    1.   Make the sauce: Heat the bacon drippings in a saucepan. Add the red onion and garlic and sauté for 1 minute. Stir in the sugar, vinegar, catsup, beer, salt, and Worcestershire sauce; reduce the heat to a simmer and continue cooking for 10 minutes.

2.   Grill the shrimp: Arrange the lime slices on one side of a prepared grill basket. Put shrimp over and around the lime and sprinkle with the red pepper flakes and paprika. Close the basket. Grill on each side for about 2–4 minutes, until the shrimp look translucent. Don't overcook shrimp as they get tough. Brush the onions with oil and sprinkle with salt and pepper. Grill for about 2 minutes on each side or until done.

3.   Place the grilled shrimp on a heated serving platter and drizzle with the sauce. Serve with the grilled onions and tortillas that have been warmed on the grill for 2–3 minutes.

4.   Have each guest place a tortilla on his or her plate, arrange shrimp on left side of the tortilla, and cover with onion slices. Roll tortilla from left to right.

Makes 8 servings (1½ cups sauce)

Serving suggestion: grilled corn on the cob (pull husks back, remove silk, replace husks, brush with oil, and grill until done to taste [1–2 minutes per side])

Fish substitutions: tuna, marlin

A fruity young cabernet sauvignon, such as Domaine St. Georges 1985 from California, will definitely stand up to the grilled flavor of the shrimp and onions, as well as the spicy sauce. *S.M.*

CHICAGO-STYLE SHRIMP

GARLIC CRUMB TOPPING

- ½ cup (¼ pound) butter or a combination of butter and margarine
- ¼ teaspoon salt
- ⅛ teaspoon cayenne pepper
- ¼ teaspoon paprika
- 3–5 cloves garlic, minced
- ¾ cup fresh bread crumbs, ground fine
- 3 tablespoons minced fresh parsley
- 4 tablespoons dry sherry

SHELLFISH

- 4 large lemons or limes, sliced thin
- 3 pounds large or jumbo shrimp, peeled and deveined

1. Make the topping: Melt the butter in a heavy skillet over medium heat. Mix in salt, cayenne, paprika, and garlic. Toss with bread crumbs, parsley, and sherry. Cook only until ingredients are combined; reserve.

2. Grill the shrimp: Use a prepared grill basket or grill screen or soaked and drained skewers. Arrange the lime slices on one side of the basket. Place shrimp over lime and secure the basket shut. If using a grill screen, arrange shrimp randomly with lime slices over screen, turning occasionally as you grill. Or thread lemon or lime slices with shrimp on skewers, turning as you grill. Cook only until the shrimp are done, approximately 4 minutes; do not overcook as shrimp tend to get tough. To serve, place the shrimp on a heated serving dish and top with the garlic crumb mixture; serve immediately.

Makes 8 servings

Serving suggestions: rolls, romaine lettuce with French dressing, fresh pineapple chunks

Serve a fruity young cabernet sauvignon, such as Domaine St. Georges 1985 from California. *S.M.*

SHRIMP WITH LOW-CALORIE SPICY TOMATO DRESSING

LOW-CALORIE SPICY TOMATO DRESSING
4   large tomatoes, peeled and chopped, including juice
1   teaspoon (or to taste) prepared white horseradish
1   small onion, minced

SHELLFISH
3   pounds large shrimp
8   10-inch-long wooden skewers
2   large oranges, sliced thin
Low-calorie margarine at room temperature

1.   Soak the skewers in water for 1 hour and drain.
2.   Make the dressing: In a bowl, combine the tomatoes, horseradish, and onion. Chill until ready to serve.
3.   Grill the shrimp: Thread the shrimp on skewers with orange slices arranged randomly. Brush with margarine. Cook on the prepared grill, turning occasionally, until shrimp are done to taste, approximately 4 minutes. Serve immediately with tomato dressing.

Makes 8 servings (2½ cups sauce)

Serving suggestions: oatmeal muffins or bread, grilled corn, fresh fruit for dessert

Serve a fruity young cabernet sauvignon, such as Domaine St. Georges 1985 from California. *S.M.*

Blue crabs that have just "busted" out of their shells become soft-shell crabs; it is part of the natural molting process. Allow two or three soft-shell crabs per person.

SOFT-SHELL CRABS WITH BASIL BUTTER

BASIL BUTTER

½   cup (¼ pound) butter or margarine, melted
1   teaspoon good-quality olive oil
¼   cup minced fresh basil leaves
4   tablespoons minced fresh parsley
¼   teaspoon cayenne pepper

SHELLFISH

24   soft-shell crabs
¾   cup sliced almonds
Basil leaves for garnish

   1.   Make the basil butter: Blend together the butter, oil, basil, parsley, and cayenne. Set aside.
   2.   Clean the crabs: Put the crabs, one at a time, on a cutting surface. Cut off the race portion of the crab. Lifting the shell easily on either side of the back, scrape off the gills. Lift the shell and remove the sand receptacle from under the mouth area. Discard all removed sections of the crab. Wash the crab and pat dry with paper toweling. (Your fishmonger might clean them for you.)

3.   Grill the crabs: Brush the crabs with some of the basil butter. Place them directly on the prepared grill or thread them onto skewers. Grill for about 3 minutes on each side, until they turn a reddish color. Be sure that the crabs are cooked through, but do not overcook them. Brush them with more basil butter and sprinkle with the almonds. Serve immediately, garnished with basil leaves.

Makes 8 servings

Serving suggestions: lime-marinated bay scallops, salad of red leaf, Boston, and romaine lettuce with chive vinaigrette, fried string potatoes

Fish substitution: sea scallops

The delicacy of the tender crabs and the light sauce call for a delicate chardonnay, such as Flora Springs 1986. *S.M.*

Somewhere in their evolution, stone crabs learned a trick that human scientists are trying their darnedest to imitate. Stone crabs, like lobsters, regenerate. If you pull off their claws and return them to the ocean, they will grow another set. Since stone crabs are often sold precooked, their grilling time will be short.

STONE CRAB CLAWS WITH PLUM DIPPING SAUCE

PLUM SAUCE

1   12-ounce jar Damson plum preserves
3   tablespoons red wine vinegar
1   teaspoon Dijon mustard
2   tablespoons light brown sugar
1   teaspoon finely grated orange zest

BREADING

1½ cups fine bread crumbs
6   tablespoons minced hazelnuts
2   tablespoons finely grated orange zest
1   tablespoon dried tarragon, crumbled
1   teaspoon ground chervil
2   tablespoons melted butter or margarine, cooled

SHELLFISH

24 stone crab claws, cracked, loose shell removed, leaving top of claw exposed
Melted butter for brushing crab claws

1. Make the sauce: Mix together the preserves, vinegar, mustard, sugar, and zest in a small, heavy saucepan. Bring the mixture to a boil and

152

reduce the heat to a simmer. Continue cooking for 4 minutes, stirring often. Cool slightly. Puree the sauce in food processor fitted with the steel blade or in a blender. Place the sauce in a serving dish and refrigerate until ready to serve. Remove the sauce from refrigerator 30 minutes before serving.

2.   Make the breading: Combine the bread crumbs, hazelnuts, zest, herbs, and butter in a small bowl. Set aside.

3.   Prepare the shellfish: Brush the claws with butter and roll in the breading, making sure the crumbs stick to the claws.

4.   Grill the shellfish: Put the crab claws on the prepared grill and cook for 1 minute. Turn the claws and continue grilling for 1 minute or until the crab meat is warm. Transfer the crab claws to a platter and serve 3 claws per person with plum dipping sauce.

Makes 8 servings (1 cup sauce)

Serving suggestions: spring green salad with goat cheese and bacon bits, chilled artichoke with dill mayonnaise, hot rolls

Fish substitution: split king crab legs

Beaujolais, light and fruity, does not overpower the crab yet stands up to the sweetness and pungency of the dipping sauce. *S.M.*

PAELLA KABOBS WITH SAFFRON RICE

This dish can be cooked outdoors completely over an open fire, as they do on the beaches of southern Spain. We have chosen to prepare the rice indoors, grill the seafood outdoors, for its special flavor, and combine the two items into a delicious treat.

Saffron is expensive but worth the cost for the taste and lovely color. A small amount will impart a golden color and a subtle taste.

16   8-inch-long wooden barbecue skewers

SAFFRON RICE

⅓   cup good-quality olive oil
1   large onion, minced
1   pound spicy sausage, skin removed, cut into ½-inch pieces
3½   cups uncooked rice
6   cups fresh or canned chicken broth
¼   teaspoon saffron threads, dissolved with the back of spoon in 2 tablespoons water
1   2-ounce jar pimiento, including liquid
2   10-ounce packages frozen peas

SHELLFISH

Enough seaweed to cover half of the grill (available at most fish markets)
1½   pounds small farm-raised mussels, cleaned and debearded
1½   pounds cherrystone clams, cleaned
1½   pounds large shrimp, shelled and deveined
1   pound sea scallops
1   cup pitted black olives
2   lemons, sliced
Good-quality olive oil for brushing shellfish
2   cloves minced garlic *or* ½ teaspoon garlic powder

1. Soak the skewers in cold water to cover for 1 hour.
2. Make the saffron rice: Heat the olive oil in a large iron skillet or a paella pan; add the onion and sausage and cook over low heat until the onion is soft, stirring occasionally. Add the rice and stir until the rice is well coated with the oil. Add the broth and saffron, avoiding the hot steam that may occur when the broth is added. Cover with a tight-fitting lid and continue cooking over low heat. After 10 minutes, stir in the pimiento and peas and cover quickly. Continue cooking about 10 more minutes, until all the liquid has been absorbed and the rice is tender.
3. Meanwhile, prepare the seafood: Spread the seaweed over the grill. Put the mussels and clams over the seaweed. Cover the grill and cook about 4 minutes or until the shellfish open. Discard any unopened shellfish.
4. Thread skewers with shrimp, scallops, olives, and lemon slices. Brush with olive oil and sprinkle with garlic.
5. Grill the kabobs, rotating every 2–3 minutes until the shellfish is cooked to your taste; do not overcook shrimp as it tends to get tough.
6. Arrange the kabobs decoratively over the saffron rice and serve immediately.

Makes 10 servings

Serving suggestions: gazpacho, Andalusian salad (greens with olives and cheese), and pineapple flan for dessert

Fish substitution: 2-inch chunks of tuna

A white rioja, Marques de Caceres 1984, provides a simple foil for the many complexities of this dish. *S.M.*

3
Side Dishes

SETTING UP THE PERFECT SALAD BAR

In the serving suggestions that accompany each recipe in this book, we almost invariably call for a green salad, because it's the perfect low-calorie, healthy, and delicious accompaniment to grilled fish—no matter what sauce is served with the fish. The next time you entertain with grilled fish as your entree, you may want to set up a salad bar for your guests. Salad bars are unique to our country and are especially appropriate for hungry and individualistic people who are used to doing things their own way without waiting for anyone to wait on them. If this kind of entertaining appeals to you, you can follow our suggestions for setting up your own salad bar. Incidentally, salad bars will work well both inside and outside. The following suggestions are meant to be just that—suggestions. Feel free to omit or add whatever you like.

The Salad Greens

You need a large bowl of at least three different kinds of mixed greens. Figure approximately 6 ounces of lettuce per person, which will be enough for large salads—the kind you want if you're only serving an appetizer, a salad, heated French bread, grilled fish, and dessert.

Include one type of green for crispness (such as iceberg or romaine), another for soft, buttery quality (such as Bibb or Boston), and a third for appearance (such as curly red, green leaf, or spinach).

The Vinaigrette

Classic French vinaigrette consists of three parts of oil to one part of vinegar. Figure either 2 or 3 teaspoons of oil per person; dieters recommend 2 teaspoons of oil per person; but salad lovers swear by 3. If you go with the 2-teaspoon formula, you'll add ⅓ cup to lettuce for eight people. If you go with the 3-teaspoon formula, you'll be using ½ cup oil for eight people.

Use only good-quality, imported olive oil (or use an olive and vegetable oil mixture). Use either red wine, white wine, malt, herb, sherry, balsamic, or fruit (such as cider or pear) vinegar. Try not to use plain white vinegar, because its flavor is uninteresting.

If you use ⅓ cup of oil, add 5¼–5½ teaspoons of vinegar. If you use ½ cup of oil add 8 teaspoons (2 tablespoons plus 2 teaspoons) of vinegar.

Preparing and Dressing the Greens

On serving day in the morning, wash the greens, then place them in a salad spinner to get rid of every bit of excess water. If you don't have a spinner, pat each individual leaf dry on both sides before storing them in a plastic bag in the refrigerator.

To ensure that the greens are crisp and, most important, dry, some hosts lay the leaves next to each other in single layers on sheets of paper toweling, then stack the leaf-covered sheets on top of each other and roll the whole thing up carefully before storing in the refrigerator. If you use this method, you'll be assured of perfect, ultra-crisp, dry leaves.

At serving time, dump the greens into an enormous bowl. (If you don't have one, use the bottom of a turkey roaster lined in plastic wrap or, lacking that, pull out one of the vegetable crisper drawers in the refrigerator and use it.)

You are going to toss the greens twice—first with the oil, then with the vinegar—the theory being that just the right amount of vinegar clings to the oil-coated leaves and the rest runs off. Add the oil first and toss carefully, coating each leaf with a thin layer; this will take a couple of minutes. Then add vinegar and toss again, slowly and carefully. Put the lettuce out at the place where you have decided the salad bar will begin. Add servers to the bowl and set out the forks, napkins, and plates (chilled in the refrigerator for a couple of hours if possible).

Guests will help themselves to the dressed leaves first, then continue down the salad bar. Additional ingredients don't need to be coated with dressing. For those die-hard fans who insist on lots of dressing, you'll set two different kinds (make one a diet dressing) at the end of the bar. Also set out additional vinegar and oil.

Additional Ingredients

Set out some or all of the following ingredients in bowls, remembering that the thinner and more finely cut the ingredients, the more elegant the salad. Whatever you decide to include, omit, or substitute for, be sure to include something pungent (like onions), something *picante* (like jalapeño peppers), and something colorful (like red tomatoes or red peppers). Each bowl should have its own serving utensil.

- Fresh tomatoes, chopped (use plum tomatoes if others aren't flavorful enough)
- Red or Vidalia onions, sliced *paper-thin* then quartered or separated into rings
- Scallions, chopped fine or snipped with scissors (or substitute finely chopped chives)
- Green and/or red peppers, cut into slivers about 1 inch long or into ultra-thin rings
- Cucumbers, peeled, seeded, and chopped
- Fresh mushrooms, sliced thin through cap and trimmed stem
- Artichoke hearts, frozen and cooked or marinated in jars and drained
- Hearts of palm, canned, cut into ¼-inch slices
- Garbanzo beans (chick-peas), canned, drained, and washed
- Bean sprouts (optional)
- Zucchini, sliced very thin
- Carrots, peeled and shredded
- Radishes, red or white, sliced thin
- Small round new potatoes, fresh, cooked and chilled
- Water chestnuts, canned, drained, and sliced thin

Garnishes

Put these sprinkle-on ingredients toward the end of the salad bar:

- Black and/or green olives, chopped coarse
- Feta cheese, crumbled
- Blue cheese, any variety, crumbled
- Parmesan or Romano cheese, *freshly* grated
- Jalepeño peppers, canned or in jars, chopped
- Bacon, fried crisp, drained, and chopped (no imitations)
- Croutons, commercially available or homemade: Rub a large frying pan with freshly cut garlic. Heat margarine or butter in the pan until sizzling. Sauté small French bread chunks until brown. Drain, allow to cook, and store uncovered.
- Chopped walnuts, chopped pecans, or pine nuts

Additional Dressings

Set out two bowls of dressing, commercially prepared if desired One should be low-calorie such as buttermilk, the other pungent, such as creamy garlic. Some hosts also set out cruets of oil and wine vinegar because someone invariably asks for more of one or the other.

Seasonings

Set out a saltshaker and a black pepper grinder. Also provide a small bowl of red pepper flakes, a small bowl of seeded lemon wedges, and a small bowl of Dijon mustard.

Hot Bread

You may want to set out heated French bread with margarine or butter at the end of the salad bar, because the crunchy, bland warmth of the hot bread is such a nice contrast to the salad. Be aware that you are repeating bread if you set out croutons, but since only a few croutons will be used, you needn't worry about it.

RATATOUILLE KABOBS

Instead of cooking all these ingredients together to make the classic French vegetable stew called ratatouille, *we first marinate the individual ingredients, then skewer them and place them on the grill.*

MARINADE

1½	cups imported mild, good-quality olive oil
½	cup fresh lemon juice
8	cloves garlic, quartered
1	medium-sized onion, quartered
1¼	teaspoons salt
1	teaspoon fresh basil leaves
½	teaspoon each fresh thyme leaves, ground coriander, and freshly ground pepper
6	dashes Tabasco sauce

VEGETABLES

1	medium eggplant-sized, peeled
3–4	thin zucchini, no thicker than 1 inch in diameter if possible
1	green bell pepper, cored, seeded, and halved lengthwise
1	red bell pepper, cored, seeded, and halved lengthwise
16	small onions, peeled (1-inch-diameter "boilers" are ideal)
16	very small plum tomatoes (*do not* use cherry tomatoes)
8	14-inch metal skewers
½	cup finely chopped fresh parsley for garnish

1. Make the marinade: Place the marinade ingredients in a blender or food processor fitted with the steel blade and process until a thick puree results. Pour the marinade into a large plastic bag.

2. Cut the eggplant in half lengthwise, then cut 24 1-inch cubes. Slice the zucchini into 1-inch-thick slices. Add the eggplant cubes and zucchini slices to the marinade.

3. Cut the green and red peppers into 16 1-inch cubes and add to the marinade.

4.   Add the peeled onions and plum tomatoes to the marinade. Secure the bag with a twister seal and turn the bag several times to make certain all vegetable surfaces touch the marinade. Place the plastic bag in a bowl and let sit at room temperature for 1 hour, turning occasionally.

5.   Pour the vegetables and marinade into the bowl. Thread vegetables alternately (see following suggested order) onto eight 14-inch skewers, beginning and ending each skewer with an eggplant cube. Reserve the marinade.

eggplant cube
red pepper square
zucchini slice (thread through skin)
onion (put on skewer widthwise, not lengthwise)
green pepper square
plum tomato (thread on skewer lengthwise, end to end)
eggplant cube

6.   Place the skewers on the prepared grill. Grill the vegetables for 8 to 10 minutes on each side, until charred, brushing with the leftover marinade every few minutes. Transfer the skewers to a serving platter and sprinkle with chopped parsley. Serve immediately.

Makes 8 servings

POTATO SALAD WITH GORGONZOLA CHEESE AND PINE NUTS

DRESSING

2 cups sour cream or sour half-and-half
6 tablespoons red wine vinegar
3 tablespoons evaporated milk
½ teaspoon sugar
½ teaspoon freshly ground pepper
Few dashes Tabasco sauce
5 ounces gorgonzola cheese, crumbled

SALAD

4 pounds (about 10 large) red potatoes
1 cup plus 1 tablespoon pine nuts
4 scallions, green part only, chopped fine
½ cup chopped fresh parsley
⅔ cup finely chopped celery (veins removed with vegetable peeler before chopping)
2½ teaspoons salt
2 tablespoons chopped fresh parsley for garnish

1. Make the dressing: Mix the dressing ingredients gently in a small bowl.

2. Make the salad: Simmer the potatoes in boiling water until they are tender enough to be pierced with a fork.

3. Meanwhile, toast the pine nuts in a large dry skillet and cook over medium heat, stirring often with a wooden spoon, until they are lightly toasted. Watch carefully; they burn quickly. You may want to pick up the skillet and shake it to prevent burning. Reserve 1 tablespoon of toasted pine nuts for garnish.

4. When the potatoes are just barely tender, remove them from the pan, drain, peel, and cut into ¼-inch-thick slices. Place in a large, flat ceramic or glass dish with raised sides or a large attractive bowl.

5. Mix the pine nuts, chopped scallions, ½ cup chopped parsley, celery, and salt in a small bowl. Sprinkle the mixture over the hot potatoes and gently toss to combine, using two rubber spatulas or wooden spoons.

6. Spoon the dressing over the potatoes and gently toss to combine. Cover with plastic wrap and let sit at room temperature for an hour before serving or cover and refrigerate for at least 2 hours. Immediately before serving, sprinkle the reserved tablespoon of toasted pine nuts and the 2 tablespoons chopped parsley over the potato salad.

Makes 12 servings (8 cups)

Serving suggestion: When you are serving simple grilled fish fillets (without a sauce), accompany them with this potato salad.

GRILLED APPLE SLICES IN A CINNAMON TOAST BASKET

This dish is easy to make and fun to serve, either as a side dish to accompany grilled fish, as a snack, or as a dessert with coffee.

1	2-pound loaf bakery white bread, unsliced
½	cup (¼ pound) butter or margarine, melted
¼	cup sugar
1	teaspoon ground cinnamon
6–8	small tart apples, cored (do not peel) and cut into ½-inch-thick rings

1. See the accompanying illustration and directions for carving the loaf of bread into a basket.

2. Preheat the oven to 350°F. Brush the entire inside of the bread basket lightly with melted butter, including the underside of the basket handle. Mix the sugar and cinnamon in a small bowl and sprinkle the inside of the basket liberally with some of the mixture. Reserve the remaining butter and cinnamon sugar.

3. Place the basket in the oven for 8–10 minutes or until it begins to crisp on the edges.

4. Meanwhile, dip the apple rings in the remaining melted butter. Arrange the rings on the grill and cook for about 4 minutes on each side or until they're slightly softened and browned. Sprinkle each grilled ring lightly with cinnamon sugar. There may be some leftover cinnamon sugar. If so, place in a small bowl and transfer to the table.

5. Place the basket on a serving tray, arrange the apple rings in the basket, and serve immediately.

Makes 8 servings

TO CARVE A BREAD BASKET

A 2-pound loaf of unsliced bakery white bread can easily be carved into a bread basket with a serrated knife. It makes a nice container for fish salad, for apple slices, and for tiny fish salad sandwiches cut into squares, triangles, and rounds.

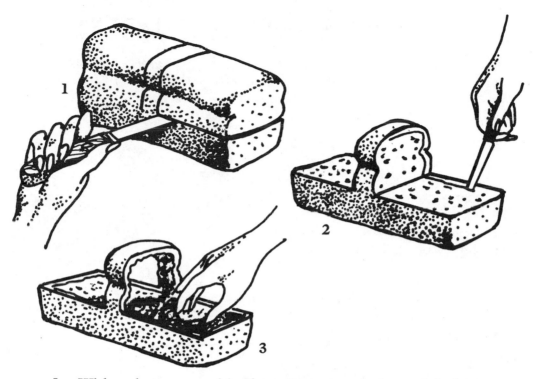

1. With a sharp serrated knife, make two vertical cuts 1 inch apart across the top of a stale 2-pound loaf of bakery white bread and continue cutting halfway through the loaf as in illustration 1. This will form the handle.

2. Beginning halfway down the loaf on one end, make a horizontal slice through the loaf up to the handle. Do the same on the other side. (Reserve the two pieces of bread for bread crumbs; see note below.)

3. Use a sharp knife to hollow out the basket and handle as in illustration 2, leaving a 1-inch border around the bread and handle. Trim all edges with large scissors to even if necessary. (Reserve the removed bread for bread crumbs; see note below).

Note: Tear the removed bread into small pieces and make bread crumbs in a blender or a food processor fitted with the steel blade. Transfer the bread crumbs to a plastic bag, secure with a twister seal, and store in the freezer until needed.

CABBAGE SLAW WITH ROTINI

This delicious cabbage/pasta slaw is made with an uncooked dressing that thickens when the vinegar and evaporated milk combine. If desired, substitute any pasta pieces such as shells for the rotini (corkscrew-shaped pasta).

DRESSING

⅓ cup sugar
2 teaspoons salt
½ teaspoon freshly ground pepper
½ cup white vinegar
3 tablespoons Dijon mustard
1 cup sour cream
1 cup evaporated milk

SALAD

8 cups (1¾ pounds) shredded cabbage
6 ounces dry rotini, cooked and chilled (2⅔ cups)
1 red bell pepper, minced fine
1 green bell pepper, minced fine
⅓ cup very finely minced onion
1 scallion, green part only, minced
⅔ cup finely chopped fresh parsley
8 ounces cream cheese, cubed (optional)

1. Make the dressing: Combine the sugar, salt, and pepper in a small bowl. Add the vinegar and stir to combine, then stir in the mustard.

2. Add the sour cream and incorporate into the mixture with a wire whisk, mixing well. Then add the evaporated milk and mix again with a wire whisk. Let sit in the refrigerator for at least 2 hours to allow the dressing to thicken.

3. At serving time, toss the salad: Combine the shredded cabbage, rotini, red and green peppers, onion, scallion, and parsley in a large bowl. (If you don't have a large enough bowl, use a small refrigerator produce drawer or a Dutch oven.) Toss the cabbage mixture with the dressing. If you are using the optional cream cheese, add it just before serving.

Makes 8–10 cups

GRILLED HERBED POLENTA SQUARES

1   teaspoon salt
1½ quarts water
1½ cups yellow cornmeal
1   teaspoon dried sage, basil, and rosemary, crumbled (in any
    proportion)
Melted butter or margarine

1.   Stir the salt into the water in a medium saucepan. Whisk in cornmeal and herbs, making sure no lumps form. Bring the mixture to a boil over medium heat, whisking constantly. Reduce the heat to a simmer and continue cooking until the polenta is thick and begins to pull away from the sides of the pan, about 20–25 minutes.

2.   Pour the polenta into a buttered 9″ × 12″ pan and chill until firm.

3.   Cut into 3-inch squares and brush with melted butter.

4.   Grill the polenta squares on the prepared grill for 1 minute. Brush with butter again, turn and continue grilling for 1–2 minutes, just until warm. Serve hot.

Makes 6–8 servings (12 pieces)

Serving suggestion: Serve with marinara sauce.

SWEET POTATO AND PINEAPPLE KABOBS

8   8-inch wooden barbecue skewers
4-5   sweet potatoes, as long, thin, and evenly shaped as possible
1   large ripe pineapple, peeled, eyes removed, cut into 1¼-inch slices
4   tablespoons melted butter or margarine
Small bowl sugar mixed with a few pinches ground cinnamon

1.   Soak the wooden barbecue skewers in water to cover for 1 hour.

2.   Boil the sweet potatoes in water to cover until they are tender enough to be pierced with a fork. Remove from water and peel. Allow to cool. Cut the potatoes into 1-inch-thick slices. You will need 24 sweet potato slices, each 1 inch wide.

3.   Cut the pineapple slices into quarters and cut away the core sections. The pineapple pieces should be about the same size as the sweet potato slices. Cut any larger pieces in half. You should end up with 32 pineapple chunks.

4.   Remove the skewers from the water and thread alternately with sweet potato and pineapple, using 4 pineapple and 3 sweet potato pieces and beginning and ending with pineapple.

5.   Brush the kabobs with melted butter. Place the skewers on the prepared grill and cook 4-5 minutes on each side. Remove from the grill and place on a serving platter. Sprinkle liberally with cinnamon sugar. Serve hot.

Makes 8 servings

REFRIED BEANS

4½ cups cooked red kidney beans, excess liquid drained and reserved
5 tablespoons bacon drippings
1 large onion, minced
4 cloves garlic, minced
1 teaspoon ground cumin
¾ teaspoon salt (to taste)
¾ teaspoon chili caribe flakes
½ teaspoon freshly ground pepper

1. Mash the beans in a food processor fitted with the steel blade or with a potato masher, using the reserved liquid as needed to make a pliable mixture. Reserve.

2. Heat the drippings in a large skillet and add the onion and garlic. Sauté, stirring occasionally until soft. Stir in the beans, cumin, salt, chili caribe flakes, and pepper. Continue cooking over medium heat until the beans are heated through and the desired thickness, adding liquid as necessary. Serve at room temperature or hot.

Makes 8 servings

4
Desserts

LADY BALTIMORE CAKE

Although credit for creating this extraordinary cake is often given to Alicia Rhett Mayberry, one of the belles of Baltimore in the early part of the 20th century, no one knows for certain where the cake originated. In 1906, novelist Owen Wister made the cake famous when he not only described it in delicious detail but also focused the action of his novel Lady Baltimore *around it. Although many versions exist, the classic Lady Baltimore Cake is a three-layer 10-inch white cake frosted with a sherry-flavored Italian meringue and filled with Italian meringue mixed with figs, nuts, and raisins. It also includes a sugar syrup that is sprinkled on the layers before frosting and filling to keep the layers moist.*

BATTER
1	cup (½ pound) butter or margarine
1¾	cups sugar
1	tablespoon baking powder
1½	teaspoons vanilla extract
3	cups sifted cake flour
1	cup milk
6	egg whites
⅛	teaspoon cream of tartar

SYRUP
¼	cup sugar
¼	cup water

FROSTING
2½	cups sugar
1	cup water
1	tablespoon light corn syrup
3	egg whites
⅛	teaspoon cream of tartar
¼	cup dry sherry (use only good-quality imported sherry)

FILLING

1 cup golden raisins
½ pound dried figs (about 12), cut into small pieces with scissors
2 cups finely chopped walnuts

1.   Make the batter: Preheat the oven to 350°F. Cream the butter in the large bowl of an electric mixer; measure out ¼ cup of the sugar and reserve to use with egg whites. Add the remaining 1½ cups sugar to the butter and beat until well creamed. Beat in the baking powder, then beat in the vanilla. Add the sifted flour alternately with the milk, beginning and ending with flour.

2.   Beat the egg whites until they hold soft peaks; with the beaters still running, add the cream of tartar and beat for another few seconds to combine. Add the reserved ¼ cup sugar. Beat until a soft meringue is made.

3.   Fold the meringue into the cake batter. Divide the batter evenly among three 10-inch round cake pans that have been well greased and lined on the bottom with greased waxed paper.

4.   Bake the layers in the preheated oven for 40–45 minutes or until the layers are lightly browned on the edges and have begun to pull away from the sides of the pan. Test the layers for doneness by inserting a toothpick in the center, then removing it and running it between your thumb and forefinger to make sure the batter is not sticky. Turn the layers onto cake racks to cool, then remove the waxed paper circles carefully from the bottoms of the layers.

5.   When the cake is completely cool, use a serrated knife to even layers carefully until they are exactly the same size.

6.   Make the syrup: Heat the sugar and water in a small skillet and simmer for 6–7 minutes. Immediately brush the layers with the hot syrup.

7.   Make the frosting and filling: Bring the sugar, water, and corn syrup to a boil. Insert a candy thermometer and heat to a simmer.

8.   While the sugar mixture simmers, place the egg whites in a clean bowl of an electric mixer and measure out the cream of tartar. When the syrup has reached 230°F, turn on the beaters. Beat the egg whites until soft peaks form, add the cream of tartar, and continue beating until stiff peaks form. Then turn off the beaters and wait for the syrup to reach 234°F.

9.   When the syrup reaches exactly 234°F, remove from the heat and place the thermometer in the sink. Turn the beaters on again and with the beaters running pour the hot syrup into the egg whites in a thin, steady

stream. When all the syrup has been added, continue beating for another minute or two; then add the sherry and beat again until well combined.

10. Measure out half the frosting and mix with the raisins, figs, and walnuts.

11. Fill and frost the cake: Tear off four waxed paper strips and lay them on the outer edges of a serving platter. Place one cake layer in the center of the plate and use one-half the filling to cover the layer completely. Top with the second layer and use the remaining filling to cover that layer completely.

12. Place the third layer on the cake. Use a spatula to cover the sides and top of the cake carefully with the frosting. Let the cake sit at room temperature for at least 4 hours before carefully pulling out the waxed paper strips.

Makes 12–16 servings

DOUBLE CHOCOLATE MADELEINES

Store these brownielike cookies in an airtight container. Madeleine pans (shell-shaped pans) are available at gourmet cooking shops and by mail (see Appendix for source).

¼ pound semisweet chocolate
¾ cup (6 ounces) butter or margarine, at room temperature
1¼ cups sifted cake flour
½ teaspoon baking powder
¼ teaspoon salt
3 eggs
⅔ cup sugar
1 teaspoon vanilla extract
6 ounces mint semisweet chocolate chips

1. Make the batter: Butter a madeleine mold, which usually has 12 depressions, and set aside.

2. Melt the chocolate in a microwave oven on HIGH for 1½–2 minutes or in the top of a double boiler over simmering water. Stir in the butter until melted.

3. Preheat the oven to 350°F. Mix together flour, baking powder, and salt. Beat the eggs in a large bowl of an electric mixer until fluffy and tripled in volume. Sprinkle the sugar over the eggs and incorporate. Fold in the cooled chocolate mixture and the vanilla.

4. Sprinkle the flour mixture over the batter and incorporate.

5. Spoon 1 tablespoon of the batter into each shell depression. Bake in the preheated oven for 12–14 minutes or until the cookies are firm to the touch. Remove the cookies from the pan and cool on a wire rack.

6. Melt the mint chocolate chips in a microwave oven on HIGH for 1½–2 minutes or in the top of a double boiler over simmering water, stirring occasionally. Dip the edge of each shell into chocolate and smooth with the tip of a knife. Or brush the edges with chocolate. Cool on a sheet of waxed paper.

Makes 36 cookies

BROWN SUGAR CHOCOLATE CAKE

BROWN SUGAR FUDGE FROSTING

- 4 cups lightly packed brown sugar
- ¼ cup light corn syrup
- 1⅓ cups milk
- ⅛ teaspoon salt
- 4½ ounces unsweetened chocolate, chopped
- ½ cup (¼ pound) butter or margarine, cut into chunks
- 2 teaspoons vanilla extract

BATTER

- 6 ounces unsweetened chocolate
- 1 cup boiling water
- 1⅓ cups (10⅔ ounces) butter or margarine
- 3 cups brown sugar
- 4 teaspoons baking powder
- 1 teaspoon baking soda
- ½ teaspoon salt
- 2 teaspoons vanilla extract
- 6 eggs
- 4 cups sifted cake flour
- 2 cups buttermilk

1. Make the frosting: Place the brown sugar, corn syrup, milk, and salt in a large, heavy-bottomed saucepan and stir to combine. Insert a candy thermometer and cook until the thermometer registers 234°F.

2. Remove from the heat and add the chocolate, stirring with a wooden spoon until well combined. Add the butter without stirring and allow it to melt on top of the chocolate, forming a protective liquid layer. Let sit for 1 hour without stirring or disturbing in any way.

3. After 1 hour, transfer the frosting to the bowl of an electric mixer and add the vanilla. Turn the beaters on and beat several minutes, until thick and spreadable. *Note:* If the frosting stiffens and becomes too dense to spread, add 2–3 teaspoons of hot water and beat until creamy enough to spread.

4.   Make the batter: Place the unsweetened chocolate in a small bowl and cover with the boiling water until melted.

5.   Preheat the oven to 350°F. Meanwhile, cream the butter until fluffy, then add the brown sugar and cream again. Add the baking powder, baking soda, and salt, beating well; then add the vanilla and beat again.

6.   Add the eggs, one at a time, beating well after each is added. Add the sifted cake flour alternately with the buttermilk in three additions, beginning and ending with flour.

7.   Divide the batter evenly among three 10-inch round cake pans that have been well greased and lined on the bottom with greased waxed paper circles cut to fit.

8.   Bake the layers for 30–35 minutes or until a toothpick inserted in the center comes out clean.

9.   Invert the layers onto wire racks (or use a cool oven rack with a book propping up each corner) and carefully peel off the waxed paper circles. Allow to cool to room temperature, then examine the layers for evenness. If they are not absolutely level, use a serrated knife to level them, shaving very thin pieces off the mounded portions little by little until the layers are level.

10.   Tear off four waxed paper strips and lay them along the edges of a cake platter. Lay one cake layer on the serving platter with the edges resting on the waxed paper strips. Spread some of the frosting over the layer. Carefully place the second cake layer on top of the first and spread frosting over this layer. Then place the third cake layer carefully on the second layer. Frost the sides of the cake, then the top. Let sit for about 2 hours at room temperature. Then carefully pull the waxed paper strips away from the bottom of the cake.

Makes 8 servings

LEMON CRUMB PIE

The food processor and the freezer combine here to allow a new kind of butter pie crust—one that's similar to a soft cookie rather than a flaky pastry. Here, the frozen butter is processed to form fine crumbs. These crumbs can then be poured into any pie pan and patted against the bottom and sides.

CRUST
1¼   cups cake flour
¼   teaspoon baking powder
⅛   teaspoon salt
½   cup (¼ pound) frozen butter or margarine, cut into small pieces
2   tablespoons sour cream
1   egg yolk

FILLING
Zest of 1 lemon, chopped fine
3   eggs
1¼   cups sugar
6   tablespoons fresh lemon juice
½   cup plus 2 tablespoons water
3   tablespoons melted butter or margarine

STREUSEL
½   cup sugar
½   cup plus 1 tablespoon flour
½   teaspoon baking powder
5   tablespoons frozen butter or margarine

1.   Make the crust: Preheat the oven to 325°F. Place all crust ingredients in a food processor fitted with the steel blade. Pulse, turning the processor on and off until the mixture resembles fine meal. Pat the crumbs onto the bottom and sides of a 9-inch pie pan. Bake the unfilled pie shell in the preheated oven for 30 minutes. Remove from the oven and allow to cool to room temperature before adding the filling.

2.   Make the filling: Preheat the oven to 400°F. Combine all the filling ingredients, mixing well. Spoon the filling into the cooled shell and bake for 15 minutes.

3. Meanwhile, make the streusel: Place all the streusel ingredients in a food processor fitted with the steel blade and pulse until fine crumbs result. When the pie has baked for 15 minutes, remove it from the oven and carefully sprinkle the top with the streusel. Return it to the oven for 20-25 minutes or until the top of the pie is golden brown. Allow to cool slightly. Serve warm, at room temperature, or chilled.

Makes 8 servings

TERRAPIN CANDIES

1   1-pound package caramels, wrappers removed
2   tablespoons milk
1   6-ounce package semisweet chocolate chips
2   cups chopped walnuts

1. Melt the caramels in the top of a double boiler over simmering water and stir in the milk. Or melt the caramels in a microwave oven in a glass bowl on HIGH for about 1½ minutes, stirring once, and add the milk.

2. Melt the chocolate chips in the top of a double boiler over simmering water or in a microwave oven in a glass bowl on HIGH for 1½ minutes or until melted.

3. Cover a cookie sheet with waxed paper. Drop ½ tablespoons of the soft caramel on waxed paper about 2 inches apart. Sprinkle with chopped walnuts, pressing slightly so that they will stick to the caramel. Drizzle melted chocolate over the walnuts in a design covering the caramel.

4. Cool the candies in a dry area until they are firm.

Makes 30 candies

WHITE CHOCOLATE CAKE WITH MILK CHOCOLATE GLAZE

BATTER

5 ounces white baking chocolate
¼ cup water
6 tablespoons butter or margarine, cut into pieces
1¼ cups sugar
2 eggs, separated
2¼ cups cake flour
1½ teaspoons baking powder
¼ teaspoon salt
¾ cup buttermilk
1 teaspoon vanilla extract
1 cup chopped almonds

GLAZE

¼ pound milk chocolate
1 tablespoon butter or margarine

1. Make the batter: Melt the white chocolate and water in a microwave oven on HIGH for 1½–2 minutes or in the top of a double boiler over simmering water; stir until smooth and let cool.

2. Preheat the oven to 350°F. Beat the butter and 1 cup of the sugar in a large bowl of an electric mixer until light. Add the egg yolks, one at a time, until incorporated.

3. Sift the flour, baking powder, and salt together. Add the flour mixture to the butter mixture, alternately with the buttermilk. Stir in the vanilla and cooled chocolate.

4. Beat the egg whites until soft peaks form. Sprinkle with the remaining sugar and continue beating until stiff peaks form. With a spatula, fold the egg whites and almonds into the batter.

5. Pour the batter into a greased 9-inch square baking pan lined with waxed paper and bake in the preheated oven for 55–60 minutes or until a wooden skewer inserted in the center of the cake comes out clean. Cool the

cake in the pan for 15 minutes. Loosen the edges of the cake and invert onto a wire rack. Set aside to cool.

    6.   Make the glaze: Melt the chocolate and butter in the top of a double boiler over simmering water. Stir until blended. Drizzle the glaze over the cake.

Makes 8–9 servings

PINEAPPLE IN PLUM WINE

This well-known Japanese favorite is easy, delicious, and refreshing. Serve this dessert with a dinner at which you've served plum wine.

1   large ripe pineapple
1   bottle real Japanese plum wine (do not use any wine labeled "imitation plum wine")

    The day before serving, peel, core, and remove the eyes from the pineapple. Cut the pineapple into bite-sized chunks and place in an attractive glass bowl. Pour in enough wine to cover the pineapple; this will probably take most of the bottle. Cover the bowl with plastic wrap and refrigerate overnight. Serve chilled in attractive glass dessert bowls.

Makes 6–8 servings

COOKIE CRUST BLUEBERRY TART

COOKIE CRUST
½ cup (¼ pound) butter or margarine, cut into small pieces
1 egg yolk
1 cup flour
¼ cup sugar

FILLING
1 quart fresh blueberries
Confectioners' sugar

1. Make the crust: Combine the crust ingredients in a food processor fitted with the steel blade. Process until the ingredients combine and a dough forms, about 10 seconds.

2. Pat the dough evenly into the bottom and up the sides of a 9- or 9½-inch tart pan with a removable bottom.

3. Fill the tart: Preheat the oven to 350°F. Wash and pick over the berries; drain dry on paper toweling. Mound the berries in the tart shell. Bake the tart in the preheated oven for 45 minutes or until the crust is done. It will be a golden brown.

4. Remove the tart from the oven and sprinkle with confectioners' sugar. Serve warm or cold. It is especially good served with rich vanilla ice cream.

Makes 8 servings

Appendix:
Mail Order Sources of
Ingredients and Equipment

Foodstuffs
338 Park Ave.
Glencoe, IL 60022
(312) 835-5105
Gourmet shop, all-purpose

Holy Land Grocery, Inc.
4806 N. Kedzie Ave.
Chicago, IL 60659
(312) 588-3306
Middle Eastern ingredients

The Oriental Food Market
2801 W. Howard St.
Chicago, IL 60645
(312) 274-2826
Oriental ingredients

Star Market
3349 N. Clark St.
Chicago, IL 60659
(312) 472-0599
Japanese ingredients

Carolyn Collins Caviar
PO Box 662
Crystal Lake, IL 60014
(815) 459-6210
American caviar and roe

Pete Casados of Casados Farms
PO Box 1269
San Juan Pueblo, NM 87103
(505) 852-2433
Chile caribe and
southwestern/Mexican ingredients

Maid of Scandinavia
3244 Raleigh Ave.
Minneapolis, MN 55416
Madeleine molds

The Chef's Catalog
3215 Commercial Ave.
Northbrook, IL 60062-1920
(312) 480-9400
Madeleine pans

INDEX

Alfredo Sauce, 80
Almond Paste, 82
Anise Butter, 94
Appetizers, 18-25
Apricot Sauce, 96

Barbecue Butter, 102
Barbecue Sauce, 102
Basil Butter, 58, 150
Black Butter Sauce, 65
Black Caviar Butter, 134
Black Olive Aioli, 78
Blueberries, Cookie Crust
    Blueberry Tart, 180
Bluefish, 8
Brown Sugar Chocolate
    Cake, 174-75
Brown Sugar Fudge
    Frosting, 174
Burrito Salsa, 70

Cabbage Slaw with Rotini,
    166
Catfish, 8, 26-30
  Catfish with Mexican Red
    Sauce, 30
  Stuffed with Couscous,
    28-29
  with Fried Onions, 26-27
Caviar Mayonnaise, 22
Champagne Sauce, 68
Chicago Sauce, 138
Chicago Style Shrimp, 148
Chilled Salmon with Red
    Caviar Mayonnaise,
    22-23

Chinese Cabbage Packets,
    76-77
Clams, 10
Cod, 8, 31-35
  Cod Steaks in Wine with
    Romesco Sauce,
    32-33
  Cod Steaks with
    Watercress Sauce and
    Watercress
    Sandwiches, 34-35
Cold Halibut Hors
    D'Oeuvres with
    Whipped Cream
    Mustard, 18-19
Cookie Crust Blueberry
    Tart, 180
Corn Relish, 90
Couscous, 28
Crab, 10. See also Soft Shell
    Crabs
Crayfish, 10

Dark Raisin Sauce, 140
Desserts, 170-80
Double Chocolate
    Madeleines, 172-73

Eggplant, 31
Entrees, 26-155

Fajita Sauce, 146
Fish Salad in a Toasted Loaf,
    142-43
Flounder, 8, 36-43

Grilled Oriental Style,
36–37
Flounder in Spinach
Packets, 38–39
Grilled Melt, 42–43
Fried Leeks, 68
Frosting, 170

Garnishes, 158
Grape Sauce, 54
Green, Louie, 7
Griffo-grill, 13
Grilled Apple Slices in a
Cinnamon Toast Basket,
164–65
Grilled Do-It-Yourself Sushi
Bar, 48–50
Grilled Dover Sole with
Herbs and Mint Butter,
104–5
Grilled Fish Sandwiches in a
Toast Basket, 145
Grilled Flounder Melt,
42–43
Grilled Herbed Polenta
Squares, 167
Grilled Mackerel in Miso
Sauce, 52–53
Grilled Mackerel with Green
Grapes, 54–55
Grilled Red Snapper
Alfredo, 80–81
Grilled Salmon with Corn
Relish, 90–91
Grilled Shad Roe on Toast
with Capers, 101
Grilled Sole Fillets with
Herbs, 107
Grilled Swordfish on Grape
Leaves, 110–11
Grilled Trout with Two
Cheeses, 117

Grilled Tuna Sandwiches,
42, 124–25
Grilled Tuna with Red
Pepper Sauce, 126–27
Grilled Whole Flounder
Oriental Style, 36–37
Grilling tips, 5–7, 11–12
Grouper, 8

Haddock, 8
Halibut, 8, 18–19, 44–47
Halibut Fillets with Miso
Sauce, 44–45
Halibut Steaks with
Cilantro and Lime
Butter, Grilled
Shallots and
Mushrooms, 46–47
Homemade Butter, 134

Ingredients and equipment,
4–5

Lady Baltimore Cake,
170–72
Lake Trout, 8, 120-21
Lake Trout on Rose Leaves
Served with Rose Butter,
120–21
Leftover fish, 142–45
Lemon Crumb Pie, 176–77
Light Raisin Sauce, 72
Lime Butter, 46
Lobster, 10
Low-Calorie Spicy Tomato
Dressing, 149

Mackerel, 8, 20–21, 48–56,
52–55
Grilled in Miso Sauce,
52–53

Grilled with Green
  Grapes, 54–55
Mackerel Appetizer
  Marinated in the
  Japanese Manner, 20–21
Magee, Shawn, 16
Mahimahi, 8, 56–57
Mahimahi Seafood
  Ranchero, 56–57
Marinade, basic recipe for,
  25
Marlin, 58–59
  Marlin with Bay Leaves
    and Basil Butter,
    58–59
Mediterranean Pita Pockets,
  31–32
Menu planning, 14–16
Mint Butter, 104
Miso Sauce, 44
Mixed Shellfish, 154–55
Monkfish, 8, 60–62
  Monkfish with Cracked
    Green Olives, 60–62
Mussels, 10

New Orleans-Style Sauce, 84

Ocean Perch with Pine Nut
  Butter Sauce, 63
Ono, 64
  Ono Grilled on a Bed of
    Tarragon Leaves, 64
Orange Roughy, 8, 65–71
  Burritos, 70–71
  Orange Roughy with Black
    Butter Sauce, 65–66
  Orange Roughy with
    Champagne Sauce,
    68–69

Orange Roughy with
  Pecan Sauce, 66–67
Oriental-Style Sea Bass, 100

Paella Kabobs with Saffron
  Rice, 154–55
Pecan Sauce, 66
Perch, 63
Pine Nut Butter Sauce, 63
Pine Nut Sauce, 108
Pineapple Plum Wine, 179
Pineapple Salsa, 85
Piping stars of sauce, how
  to, 19
Pistachio Paste, 132
Plum Sauce, 152
Pollack, 8
Pomegranate Sauce, 98
Pompano, 8, 72–73
  Pompano with Light
    Raisin Sauce, 72–73
Potato Salad with
  Gorgonzola Cheese and
  Pine Nuts, 162–63

Rainbow Trout, 118–19
Ranchero Salsa, 56
Ratatouille Kabobs, 160–61
Red Pepper Sauce, 126
Red Sauce, 30
Red Snapper, 8, 74–85
  Grilled Alfredo, 80–81
  Red Snapper Fillets with
    Gorgonzola, 74–75
  Red Snapper New Orleans-
    Style, 84
  Red Snapper with
    Marzipan, 82–83
  Red Snapper with
    Pineapple Salsa, 85

Red Snapper with Spanish
    Wine Butter and Black
    Olive Aioli, 78–79
Redfish, 8
Refried Beans, 169
Regrilled Fish Patties, 144
Rockfish, 8, 86–88
    Rockfish Fillets with
        Saffron Beurre Blanc,
        88
    Rockfish with White Wine
        Sauce, 86–87
Romesco sauce, 32
Rose Butter, 120
Roughy Burritos, 70–71

Saffron Beurre Blanc, 88
Saffron Rice, 154
St. Peter's Fish on the Grill,
    118–19
Salad bar, 156–59
Salad greens, 156
Salmon, 8, 22–23, 89–93
    Chilled with Red Caviar
        Mayonnaise, 22–23
    Grilled Salmon with Corn
        Relish, 90–91
    Salmon Patties on the
        Grill, 92–93
    Salmon Quenelles in
        Flounder, 40–41
    Stuffed Salmon with Wild
        Mushrooms, 89–90
Scallops, 10
Scrod, 94–99
    Scrod Fillets with Apricot
        Sauce, 96–97
    Scrod Fillets with
        Pomegranate Sauce,
        98–99

Scrod with Anise Butter,
    94–95
Sea Bass, 8, 100
Serpentine Swordfish Strips,
    112–13
Sesame Seed Sauce, 114–15
Shad, 8
Shad Roe, 101
    Grilled on Toast with
        Capers, 101
Shark, 8, 102–3
    Shark with Barbecue
        Butter, 102–3
Shellfish, 146–55
Shiitake Mushrooms, 136
Shrimp, 146–49
    Shrimp Fajitas, 146–47
    Shrimp with Low-Calorie
        Spicy Tomato
        Dressing, 149
Side dishes, 156–69
Skewered Fish Sausage
    Appetizer, 24–25
Smelt, 8
Soft-shell Crabs, 150–51
    Soft-shell Crabs with Basil
        Butter, 150–51
Sole, 8, 104–9
    Grilled Sole Fillets with
        Herbs, 107
    Grilled with Herbs and
        Mint Butter, 104–5
    Sole with Cider and
        Grilled Pear Slices,
        106
    Sole with Pine Nut Sauce,
        108–9
Solomon, Leonard, 16
Spanish Wine Butter, 78
Spinach Mousse, 38

Squid, 10
Stone Crab Claws, 152–53
  Stone Crab Claws with
      Plum Dipping Sauce,
      152–53
Stuffed Catfish with
    Couscous, 28–29
Stuffed Salmon with Wild
    Mushrooms, 89–90
Sushi Bar, 48–50
Sushi Rice, 51
Sweet Potato and Pineapple
    Kabobs, 168
Swordfish, 8, 110–13
  Grilled on Grape Leaves,
      110–11

Temaki-Sushi, 50
Terrapin Candies, 177
Toast Basket, 34, 145,
    164–65
Toasted Loaf, 142. *See also*
    Toast basket
Trout, 114–23
  Grilled with Two Cheeses,
      117
  Trout in a Bacon Blanket,
      122–23
  Trout with Sesame Seed
      Sauce, 114–15
Tuna, 8, 124–27
  Grilled Sandwiches, 42,
      124–25
  Grilled with Red Pepper
      Sauce, 126–27

Turbot, 8, 128–30
  Turbot Fillets with
      Turkish Hazelnut
      Sauce, 128–29
  Turbot with Cumin, 130

Vinaigrette, 156–57

Watercress Sauce, 34
Whipped Cream Mustard
    Sauce, 18
White Chocolate Cake with
    Milk Chocolate Glaze,
    178–79
White Wine Sauce, 86
Whitefish, 8, 24, 131–41
  Whitefish Fillets with
      Black Caviar Butter,
      134–35
  Whitefish Fillets with
      Dark Raisin Sauce,
      140–41
  Whitefish Fillets with
      Pistachio, Garnished
      with Skewered Fruit,
      131–33
  Whitefish with Chicago
      Sauce, 138–39
  Whitefish with Lichees
      and Shiitake
      Mushrooms, 136–37
Wild Mushroom Stuffing,
    89
Wine with grilled fish,
    15–16